The Vegan Instant Pot Duo Crisp Air Fryer Cookbook

250 Days Easy and Delicious Vegan Friendly Recipes for

Smart People to Master Instant Pot Duo Crisp Air Fryer

Jeffrey R. Alexander

Copyright© 2021 By Jeffrey R. Alexander All Rights Reserved

This book is copyright protected. It is only for personal use. You cannot amend, distribute, sell, use, quote or paraphrase any part of the content within this book, without the consent of the author or publisher.

Under no circumstances will any blame or legal responsibility be held against the publisher, or author, for any damages, reparation, or monetary loss due to the information contained within this book, either directly or indirectly.

Disclaimer Notice:

Please note the information contained within this document is for educational and entertainment purposes only. All effort has been executed to present accurate, up to date, reliable, complete information. No warranties of any kind are declared or implied. Readers acknowledge that the author is not engaged in the rendering of legal, financial, medical or professional advice. The content within this book has been derived from various sources. Please consult a licensed professional before attempting any techniques outlined in this book.

By reading this document, the reader agrees that under no circumstances is the author responsible for any losses, direct or indirect, that are incurred as a result of the use of the information contained within this document, including, but not limited to, errors, omissions, or inaccuracies.

Table of content

Introduction 1

Chapter 1 Breakfasts 2

    Healthy Chia and Blueberry Oats 2

    Crunchy Peanut Butter Granola Bars 2

    Apple Breakfast Risotto 3

    Creamy Rice Pudding 3

    Amaranth Banana Bread 4

    Healthy Instant Pot Granola 4

    Loaded Sweet Potato Breakfast 5

    Spicy Tempeh Breakfast "Sausage" 5

    Pecan Butter Toast 6

    Cranberry Muffins 7

    Corn Buttermilk Bread 7

    Pancake with Vanilla 8

    Blueberry Muffins 9

    Pecan Bread 10

    Bread with Butter 10

    Cherry Tomato Cheese Frittata 11

    Oatmeal and Pecan Bars 12

    Mango Yogurt Parfaits with Walnut 12

Chapter 2 Snacks and Appetizers 13

    Creamy Corn Polenta 13

    Classic Baba Ghanoush 13

    Thai Red Curry Mashed Chickpea 14

Cauliflower and Tomato Queso.. 14

Chinese Sesame Baby Carrots... 15

Potato French Fries.. 15

Cauliflower Bites.. 16

Rice Cereal with Dill.. 17

Banana with Peanut... 17

Pasta Chips... 18

Cashews with Molasses... 18

Chickpeas with Salt... 19

Radish Chips... 19

Panko Artichoke Balls... 20

Chapter 3 Beans and Grains... 20

Almond Green Beans... 20

Hummus... 21

Indian Cumin Rice... 21

Creamy Jasmine Rice... 22

Creamy Pumpkin Risotto... 22

Beans with Tomato Sauce.. 23

Bean and Corn Taco Bowls.. 23

Bean Rice Stuffed Bell Peppers.. 24

Pineapple Brown Rice Bake... 25

Chapter 4 Soups and Stews.. 26

Paprika Carrot Soup.. 26

Easy Creamy Tomato Basil Soup.. 26

Leek and Potato Soup.. 27

Coconut Curry Lentil and Kale Soup..27

Easy Swiss Chard Stem Soup..28

Dill Celery Soup...28

Mushroom Barley Soup...29

Coconut Chickpea and Mushroom Stew...30

Peas and Potato Stew..30

Chapter 5 Vegetables and Sides..31

Cauliflower and Millet Mash..31

Easy Rosemary Red Potatoes..31

Garlicky Steamed Broccoli...32

Garlicky White Beets...32

Rosemary Carrots..33

Garlicky Boiled Bok Choy...33

Coconut Cauliflower Mash..34

Citrus Brussels Sprouts..34

Avocado Fries...35

Parsnip with Cinnamon..35

Squash Seeds with Tamari...36

Yucca Root..37

Eggplants with Tahini Sauce...37

Mushroom with Sauce..38

Zucchini and Squash Ratatouille..38

Green Beans with Sesame..39

Okra with Paprika...40

Panko Pickles..40

Onion Rings with Aquafaba 41

Potato Truffle 42

Dill Carrot 42

Chapter 6 Vegetable Mains 43

Thyme Sweet Potato Mash 43

Mushroom Risotto with Arborio Rice 43

Spicy and Sweet Braised Red Cabbage 44

Mashed Root Vegetables 45

Sesame-Garlic Green Beans 45

Classic Brazilian Potato Curry 46

Cauliflower Butternut Squash 47

Steamed Vegetables 47

Tofu Steaks with Paprika 48

Tomato Cheese Sandwiches 48

Spinach Cheese Calzones 49

Cheese Stuffed Potato 50

Eggplant Cheese Casserole 50

Tater Tot Casserole with Cheese 51

Pineapple Brown Rice Bake 52

Chapter 7 Salads 52

Sweet Potato Salad with Parsley 52

Apple and Celery Barley Salad 53

Blueberry Wheat Berry Salad 53

Pomegranate Brussels Sprout Salad 54

Beet and Carrot Salad 55

    Spinach Veggie Burger Salad..55

    Pecan and Apple Salad..56

    Squash and Asparagus Salad...57

    Corn and Black Bean Salad...57

    Crabless Cake Salad with Pineapple..58

Chapter 8 Desserts..59

    Cinnamon Balls...59

    Apple Pie..59

    Fudgy Chocolate Brownies...60

    Lemon Blueberry Cheesecake... 61

    Pear and Apple Smoothie..61

    Rhubarb and Strawberry Compote... 62

    Simple Peppermint Hot Chocolate..62

    Vanilla Rice Pudding with Cherries.. 63

    Chocolate Butter Cookie...63

    Cherry Tomatoes..64

    Vanilla Yogurt Cake...64

    Peach Yogurt Pudding Cake.. 65

    Chocolate and Banana Rolls...66

    Peach Butter Cobbler.. 66

    Cake with Cocoa...67

Chapter 9 Staples, Sauces and Dips... 67

    White Sauce...67

    Red Pepper Sauce...68

    Fresh Garden Tomato Salsa...68

Artichoke-Spinach Dip 69

Instant Pot Soy Yogurt 70

Onion Cream 70

Coco Whip with Vanilla 71

Cauliflower Chorizo 71

Chickpea Rolls with Thyme 72

Appendix 1 Measurement Conversion Chart 73

Appendix 2 Instant Pot Cooking Timetable 74

Appendix 3 Instant Pot Cooking Timetable 75

Appendix 4 Air Fryer Cooking Chart 76

Appendix 5 Air Fryer Cooking Chart 77

Introduction

When I first started my food blog nearly 10 years ago, I had no intention of moving in a primarily plant-based direction. Though I had vegan friends, I thought surely they were starving, protein deficient, and no longer enjoying the delicious foods I was passionate about. Years later, I began to do my own research, reading the science from plant-based doctors such as Dr. Michael Greger, and following strong, thriving, plant-based athletes. I learned that it's possible to eat a satisfying plant-based diet while maintaining balanced nutrition. Not only that, but I learned that vegan dishes could still contain all the umami, creaminess, textures, and flavor that omnivores enjoy. As a lifelong animal lover, it's a diet with which I'm a lot more comfortable! I'm thrilled now to be helping others fall in love with nourishing, whole plant foods that are a bit gentler on most bodies, animals, and the earth.

as somewhat of a minimalist, I find that few gadgets or appliances get me excited or feel like a necessity. My instant pot duo crisp air fryer is one of those rare appliances that was a total game changer—in so many ways. It made healthy cooking easier and quicker, batch-cooking a breeze, and trying new foods much more fun because they took less time to cook.

As a busy mom and plant-based home chef. Rice, whole grains, and legumes that traditionally take hours to soak and cook are now a breeze. I love that I no longer use cans of beans or plastic-wrapped, pre-cooked rice. The Instant Pot duo crisp air fryer has made plant-based cooking healthier, easier, quicker, cheaper, and more eco-friendly.

My goal with this book is to help you make fast, delicious vegan meals that maximize nutrition using your instant pot duo crisp air fryer. All the recipes in this book have five things in common:

- They can be cooked entirely in your instant pot duo crisp air fryer.
- They are vegan.
- They are easy to make.
- They use fresh, wholesome ingredients.
- They require only five core ingredients.

Oh, and one other thing: These recipes all taste good; otherwise, we wouldn't eat them!

So, dig in. This cookbook is perfect for anyone who is pressed for time and searching for healthy, economical, and tasty plant-based meals.

Chapter 1 Breakfasts

Healthy Chia and Blueberry Oats

Prep time: 2 minutes | Cook time: 12 minutes | Serves 4 to 6

2 cups steel-cut oats

4½ cups water

½ to 1 cup coconut milk

2 tablespoons agave, or maple syrup (optional)

¼ teaspoon salt (optional)

¼ to ½ cup chia seeds

1 cup fresh blueberries

1 cup chopped walnuts

1. Stir together the oats and water into the pressure cooker. 2. Close and lock the pressure cooker lid. Select the Pressure Cook and set the cooking time for 12 minutes at High Pressure. Press Start. 3. Once cooking is complete, do a natural pressure release for 10 minutes, then release any remaining pressure. Carefully open the lid. 4. Add the milk and stir in the agave and salt (if desired). Serve topped with the chia seeds, blueberries, and walnuts.

Crunchy Peanut Butter Granola Bars

Prep time: 5 minutes | Cook time: 20 minutes | Serves 10

1 cup quick-cooking oats

½ cup all-natural peanut butter

⅓ cup pure maple syrup

1 tablespoon extra-virgin olive oil

¼ teaspoon fine sea salt

⅓ cup dried cranberries or raisins

½ cup raw pumpkin seeds

1 cup water

1. Line a 7-inch round pan with parchment paper. 2. Combine the oats, peanut butter, maple syrup, olive oil, and salt in a large bowl and stir well. Fold in the dried cranberries and pumpkin seeds, then scrape the batter into the prepared pan. Use a spatula to press the batter evenly into the bottom of the pan. 3. Pour the water into the pressure cooker and insert a trivet. Place the pan on the trivet.

Cover the pan with another piece of parchment to protect the granola bars from condensation. 4. Close and lock the pressure cooker lid. Select the Pressure Cook and set the cooking time for 20 minutes at High Pressure. Press Start. 5. Once cooking is complete, do a natural pressure release for 10 minutes, then release any remaining pressure. Carefully open the lid. 6. Remove the trivet and let the granola cool completely in the pan. Cut the cooled granola into 10 pieces and serve.

Apple Breakfast Risotto

Prep time: 10 minutes | Cook time: 12 minutes | Serves 4 to 6

2 tablespoons vegan butter

1½ cups Arborio rice

2 apples, cored and sliced

3 cups plant-based milk

1 cup apple juice

⅓ cup brown sugar

1½ teaspoons cinnamon powder

Salt to taste

½ cup dried cherries

1. Select Sauté and melt the butter. 2. Add rice, stir and cook for 5 minutes. 3. Add the remaining ingredients, except the cherries, to the pressure cooker. Stir well. 4. Close and lock the pressure cooker lid. Select the Pressure Cook and set the cooking time for 6 minutes at High Pressure. Press Start. 5. When the timer beeps, perform a natural pressure release for 6 minutes, then release any remaining pressure. Carefully remove the lid. 6. Stir in the cherries and close the lid. Let sit for 5 minutes. Serve warm.

Creamy Rice Pudding

Prep time: 15 minutes | Cook time: 10 minutes | Serves 3

1 cup plant-based milk

½ cup basmati rice

½ cup coconut cream

¾ cup water

2 tablespoons maple syrup

1 teaspoon vanilla extract

Pinch of sea salt

1. Combine all the ingredients into the pressure cooker. 2. Close and lock the pressure cooker lid. Select the Pressure Cook and set the cooking time for 10 minutes at High Pressure. Press Start. 3. When the timer beeps, perform a natural pressure release for 10 minutes, then release any remaining pressure. Carefully remove the lid and stir. 4. Serve warm.

Amaranth Banana Bread

Prep time: 5 minutes | Cook time: 4 minutes | Serves 4

1 cup amaranth

2 cups sliced bananas

2 ½ cups vanilla-flavored rice milk

2 tablespoons brown sugar

½ teaspoon nutmeg

½ teaspoon cinnamon

¼ teaspoon salt

½ cup chopped walnuts

1. Combine all the ingredients, except for the walnuts, into the pressure cooker. 2. Close and lock the pressure cooker lid. Select the Pressure Cook and set the cooking time for 4 minutes at High Pressure. Press Start. 3. Once cooking is complete, do a natural pressure release for 10 minutes, then release any remaining pressure. Carefully open the lid. 4. Stir in the walnuts before serving.

Healthy Instant Pot Granola

Prep time: 10 minutes | Cook time: 4 hours | Makes about 3½ cups

2½ tablespoons melted coconut oil, plus more for greasing

1 cup old-fashioned rolled oats

½ cup raw pumpkin seeds

½ cup raw, hulled sunflower seeds

½ cup roughly chopped raw pecans

⅓ cup hemp seeds

1 teaspoon coconut sugar

½ teaspoon ground cinnamon

⅛ teaspoon sea salt

2½ tablespoons pure maple syrup

1. Lightly grease the bottom of the pressure cooker with coconut oil. 2. In a medium bowl, stir together the oats, pumpkin seeds, sunflower seeds, pecans, hemp seeds, coconut sugar, cinnamon, and salt. 3. Drizzle 2½ tablespoons of

coconut oil and maple syrup over the oat mixture. Toss with a spatula until well incorporated. 4. Transfer the mixture to the greased pressure cooker. 5. Close and lock the pressure cooker lid. Select the Slow Cook mode and set the cooking time for 4 hours at Low Pressure. Press Start. Gently stir the mixture halfway through the cooking time. 6. When the timer beeps, perform a natural pressure release for 10 minutes, then release any remaining pressure. Carefully remove the lid. 7. Let the granola cool completely into the pressure cooker and then stir. Serve immediately.

Loaded Sweet Potato Breakfast

Prep time: 2 minutes | Cook time: 12 minutes | Serves 2

1 medium sweet potato, rinsed and patted dry

1 cup water

Pinch of ground cinnamon

2 tablespoons almond butter

¼ cup slivered toasted almonds

2 tablespoons hemp seeds

1. Pierce the sweet potato all over with a fork. 2. Pour the water into the pressure cooker and insert a trivet. Place the sweet potato on the trivet. 3. Close and lock the pressure cooker lid. Select the Pressure Cook and set the cooking time for 12 minutes at High Pressure. Press Start. 4. When the timer beeps, perform a natural pressure release for 10 minutes, then release any remaining pressure. Carefully open the lid and make sure the sweet potato is fork-tender. If not, Close and lock the pressure cooker lid and cook for another 3 minutes, or until tender. 5. Remove the potato with tongs. Cut it in half lengthwise and place on two serving plates. Sprinkle with a pinch of cinnamon and drizzle with almond butter. Serve topped with the almonds and hemp seeds.

Spicy Tempeh Breakfast "Sausage"

Prep time: 12 minutes | Cook time: 8 minutes | Serves 4 to 6

1 tablespoon olive oil

1 (8-ounce / 227-g) package unflavored tempeh

2 teaspoons vegan Worcestershire

sauce

1½ teaspoons smoked paprika

1 teaspoon garlic powder

1 teaspoon onion powder

1 teaspoon dried sage

½ teaspoon dried oregano

½ teaspoon salt, plus more as needed

¼ teaspoon freshly ground black pepper

Pinch chili powder

1 cup water

1. Select Sauté and heat the olive oil until it shimmers. 2. Crumble the tempeh into the hot oil and stir to coat. 3. Add the Worcestershire sauce, paprika, garlic powder, onion powder, sage, oregano, salt, pepper, and chili powder. Continue to sauté, stirring as needed, for an additional 6 to 7 minutes. 4. Turn off the pressure cooker and pour in the water. Use your spoon to scrape up any bits of flavor that have stuck to the bottom of the cooker. Stir well. 5. Close and lock the pressure cooker lid. Select the Pressure Cook and set the cooking time for 3 minutes at High Pressure. Press Start. 6. Once cooking is complete, do a quick pressure release. Carefully open the lid. 7. Select the Sauté mode again and allow the remaining liquid to cook off. Taste and season with more salt, as needed.

Pecan Butter Toast

Prep time: 15 minutes | Cook time: 9 minutes | Serves 4

2 tablespoons egg replacer

⅔ cup coconut milk

1 teaspoon vanilla

4 slices French bread

⅓ cup packed brown sugar

¼ cup vegan butter

⅔ cup chopped pecans

¼ teaspoon cinnamon

1. In a large, shallow bowl, whisk together the egg replacer, milk, and vanilla until smooth. 2. Place the French bread slices into the bowl and let sit for 1 minute. Then turn the bread and let sit until you're ready to cook. 3. In a small saucepan over low heat, combine the brown sugar and butter and heat until melted, stirring occasionally. 4. In a small bowl, toss the pecans with the cinnamon. 5. Remove the bread from the egg mixture and place in the air fryer basket; you may need to do this in two batches. Drizzle the brown sugar mixture over the bread and top with the pecans. 6. Close and lock the air fryer lid. Select

Bake, set temperature to 350°F (177°C), and set time to 7 to 9 minutes. Press Start. It will be done until the French toast is golden brown and crisp. Serve.

Cranberry Muffins

Prep time: 15 minutes | Cook time: 14 minutes | Serves 4

½ cup all-purpose flour	1 tablespoon egg replacer
2 tablespoons whole-wheat flour	¼ cup coconut milk
½ teaspoon baking powder	1 teaspoon vanilla
2 tablespoons brown sugar	2 tablespoons vegetable oil
3 tablespoons quick-cooking oats	⅓ cup dried cranberries
Pinch sea salt	Nonstick baking spray containing flour

1. In a medium bowl, combine the all-purpose and whole-wheat flours, baking powder, brown sugar, oats, and salt and mix. 2. In a small bowl or a measuring cup, beat together the egg replacer, milk, vanilla, and oil until combined. 3. Add the egg mixture to the dry ingredients all at once and stir just until combined. 4. Stir in the cranberries. 5. Spray four silicone muffin cups with the baking spray. Divide the batter among them, filling each two-thirds full. 6. Place the muffin cups in the air fryer basket and the basket in the air fryer. Close and lock the air fryer lid. Select Bake, set temperature to 325°F (163°C), and set time to 12 to 14 minutes. Press Start. It will be done until the muffins are browned and the tops spring back when you touch them lightly with your finger. 7. Let the muffins cool on a wire rack for 10 to 15 minutes before serving.

Corn Buttermilk Bread

Prep time: 15 minutes | Cook time: 22 minutes | Serves 4

Nonstick baking spray containing flour

⅔ cup yellow cornmeal

½ cup all-purpose flour

1 teaspoon baking powder

½ teaspoon baking soda

¼ teaspoon sea salt

½ cup shredded vegan Cheddar cheese

1 cup buttermilk

2 tablespoons egg replacer

¼ cup vegan butter, melted

1 tablespoon honey

1. Spray a 6-inch round pan with the baking spray and set aside. 2. Combine the cornmeal, flour, baking powder, baking soda, and salt in a medium bowl. Add the cheese and toss to coat. 3. In a glass measuring cup, combine the buttermilk, egg replacer, butter, and honey until smooth. Add this to the flour mixture and stir just until combined. 4. Spread the batter into the prepared pan. 5. ut the pan in the air fryer basket. Close and lock the air fryer lid. Select Bake, set temperature to 350°F (177°C), and set time to 17 to 22 minutes. Press Start. It will be done until the corn bread is golden brown and a toothpick inserted in the center comes out clean. Let cool on a wire rack for 15 minutes before cutting into four wedges to serve.

Pancake with Vanilla

Prep time: 10 minutes | Cook time: 16 minutes | Serves 2

½ cup unbleached all-purpose flour

2 tablespoons coconut sugar

1 tablespoon baking powder

1 to 2 pinch sea salt

½ cup soymilk or other nondairy milk

1 tablespoon applesauce

¼ teaspoon vanilla extract

1 to 2 spritzes extra-virgin olive oil spray

1. Combine the flour, sugar, baking powder, and salt in a mixing bowl. Slowly whisk in the milk, applesauce, and vanilla extract. 2. Grease an 8-inch springform pan (or an oven-safe dish of your choice) with the olive oil spray. 3. Pour the

batter into the prepared pan. Place the pan into air fryer basket. Close and lock the air fryer lid. Select Bake, set temperature to 330°F (166°C), and set time to 10 minutes. Press Start. Check for doneness by inserting a toothpick into the center, it should come out dry. Cook for an additional 2 to 4 minutes as needed.

Blueberry Muffins

Prep time: 15 minutes | Cook time: 20 minutes | Makes 8 muffins

1½ teaspoons distilled white vinegar

½ cup almond milk

1 tablespoon flaxseed meal

2 tablespoons water

1 cup all-purpose white flour

¼ cup coconut sugar

1 teaspoon baking powder

½ teaspoon baking soda

⅛ teaspoon salt

2 tablespoons coconut oil

½ teaspoon pure vanilla extract

½ cup fresh blueberries

8 foil muffin cups

Cooking spray

1. In a measuring cup, add the vinegar. 2. Add enough almond milk to fill to ½ cup. 3. In a small bowl, mix the flaxseed meal and water. 4. In a large bowl, stir together the flour, sugar, baking powder, soda, and salt. 5. Warm the coconut oil just enough to liquefy it. Pour it into the bowl with the flaxseed meal. 6. Add the almond milk and vanilla and stir together. 7. Pour the liquids over the dry ingredients and stir just until moistened. Do not beat. 8. Gently fold in the blueberries. 9 Remove the liners from 8 foil muffin cups and spray the cups with cooking spray. 10. Divide the batter among 8 muffin cups and place 4 muffin cups in the air fryer basket. 11. Close and lock the air fryer lid. Select Bake, set temperature to 330°F (166°C), and set time to 9 to 10 minutes. Press Start. 12. Repeat with the 4 remaining muffins.

Pecan Bread

Prep time: 25 minutes | Cook time: 20 to 25 minutes | Serves 8

3 tablespoons coconut sugar

1 cup lukewarm water

1 (¼-ounce / 7 g) package rapid-rise yeast

1⅓ cups whole-grain white wheat flour

2 teaspoons light olive oil

½ teaspoon salt

2 teaspoons cinnamon

½ cup chopped pecans

Oil for misting or cooking spray

1. In a medium bowl, stir together the coconut sugar and water. 2. Stir in the yeast. 3. Add the flour, oil, salt, and cinnamon and stir until well blended. 4. Stir in the pecans. You will have a thick batter rather than a stiff dough. 5. Spray the air fryer baking pan and pour the batter into it. 6. Set aside to rise for 15 minutes. 7. Place the pan into air fryer basket. 8. Close and lock the air fryer lid. Select Bake, set temperature to 360°F (182°C), and set time to 20 to 25 minutes. Press Start. It will be done until a toothpick pushed into the center comes out with soft crumbs clinging to it.

Bread with Butter

Prep time: 15 minutes | Cook time: 10 minutes | Serves 4

Nonstick baking spray containing flour

1 cup all-purpose flour

¼ cup whole-wheat flour

1 tablespoon brown sugar

1 teaspoon baking powder

¼ teaspoon sea salt

6 tablespoons unsalted vegan butter, melted, divided

5 tablespoons coconut milk

¼ cup granulated sugar

1½ teaspoons cinnamon

1. Spray a 6-by-3-inch round pan with the baking spray and set aside. 2. In a small bowl, combine the all-purpose flour, whole-wheat flour, brown sugar, baking powder, and salt. 3. Stir in 3 tablespoons of melted butter and the milk and mix until a dough forms. 4. Divide the dough into 16 balls. 5. Combine the granulated sugar and cinnamon on a plate. Place the remaining 3 tablespoons of melted butter in a shallow bowl. 6. Dip the dough balls into the butter, then roll them in the cinnamon-sugar mixture to coat. As you work, drop the sugared dough balls into the prepared pan. Make sure the dough balls touch one another. 7. Place the pan in the air fryer basket. Close and lock the air fryer lid. Select Bake, set temperature to 350°F (177°C), and set time to 6 to 10 minutes. Press Start. It will be done until the bread is deep golden brown. 8. Let cool on a rack for 3 minutes, then turn the pan over to remove the bread. Enjoy!

Cherry Tomato Cheese Frittata

Prep time: 15 minutes | Cook time: 15 minutes | Serves 3

1 tablespoon unsalted vegan butter, at room temperature

4 tablespoons egg replacer

¼ cup vegan Ricotta cheese

¼ cup coconut milk

1 teaspoon dried Italian seasoning

Pinch sea salt

2 scallions, chopped

1 garlic clove, minced

⅓ cup chopped cherry tomatoes, drained

½ cup shredded vegan Provolone cheese

¼ cup grated vegan Parmesan cheese

1. Grease a 7-inch round pan with the butter and set aside. 2. In a medium bowl, beat the eggs with the Ricotta, milk, Italian seasoning, and salt. Pour this into the prepared pan. 3. Arrange the scallions, garlic, and tomatoes on the egg replacer. Top with the cheeses. 4. Put the pan in the air fryer basket. Close and lock the air fryer lid. Select Bake, set temperature to 350°F (177°C), and set time to 12 to 15 minutes. Press Start. Serve.

Oatmeal and Pecan Bars

Prep time: 5 minutes | Cook time: 7 to 9 minutes | Serves 2

Oatmeal

Oil for misting or cooking spray

Shredded coconut

Finely chopped pecans

Maple syrup for serving

1. Prepare the oatmeal according to the package directions. 2. While the oatmeal is still warm, pour it into a square or rectangular baking pan. It should be about ½-inch thick. If thicker than that, transfer some of it into another pan. 3. Chill several hours or overnight, until the oatmeal feels cold and firm. 4. When ready to cook, cut the oatmeal into 3-inch to 4-inch squares. 5. Cut each square in half to make rectangles or triangles. 6. Mist the bottoms of the oatmeal slices with oil or cooking spray. 7. Sprinkle the tops lightly with coconut and chopped pecans, pressing them in gently, then spray the tops with oil. 8. Place the slices in the air fryer basket in a single layer. Close and lock the air fryer lid. Select Bake, set temperature to 390°F (199°C), and set time to 7 to 9 minutes. Press Start. It will be done until the tops turn brown and crispy. 9. Transfer the bars to serving plates. If any toppings fall off during cooking, sprinkle them over the bars and serve them hot with maple syrup.

Mango Yogurt Parfaits with Walnut

Prep time: 5 minutes | Cook time: 10 minutes | Serves 1

⅔ cup walnuts

Pinch of kosher salt

¼ teaspoon ground cinnamon

1 tablespoon maple syrup

4 cups coconut milk yogurt

2 large mangoes, peeled and diced

1. In a small bowl, combine the walnuts, salt, cinnamon, and maple syrup. Toss

well to coat.Place the walnut mixture in a baking dish. 2. Place the dish in the fryer basket. Close and lock the air fryer lid. Select Bake, set temperature to 320°F (160°C), and set time to 10 minutes. Press Start. Toss once halfway through. 3. Remove the dish from the fryer basket and pour the nuts onto a piece of parchment paper. Allow them to cool completely. 4. In 4 parfait glasses, alternate layers of yogurt, mango, and nuts. Refrigerate for 5 minutes before serving.

Chapter 2 Snacks and Appetizers

Creamy Corn Polenta

Prep time: 5 minutes | Cook time: 10 minutes | Serves 4

3½ cups water

½ cup coarse polenta

½ cup fine yellow cornmeal

1 cup corn kernels

1 teaspoon dried thyme

1 teaspoon salt

1. Add all the ingredients to the pressure cooker and stir to combine. 2. Close and lock the pressure cooker lid. Select the Pressure Cook and set the cooking time for 10 minutes on High Pressure. Press Start. When the timer goes off, do a quick pressure release. Carefully open the lid. 3. Serve warm.

Classic Baba Ghanoush

Prep time: 10 minutes | Cook time: 11 minutes | Serves 4 to 6

1 tablespoon sesame oil

1 large eggplant, peeled and diced

4 cloves garlic, peeled and minced

½ cup water

3 tablespoons fresh Italian flat-leaf parsley

½ teaspoon salt

2 tablespoons fresh lemon juice

2 tablespoons tahini

1 tablespoon extra-virgin olive oil

1. Press the Sauté button on the pressure cooker and heat the sesame oil. Add the

eggplant and sauté for about 5 minutes, or until it begins to soften. Add the garlic and sauté for 30 seconds. Pour in the water. 2. Close and lock the pressure cooker lid. Select the Pressure Cook and set the cooking time for 6 minutes on High Pressure. Press Start. When the timer goes off, do a quick pressure release. Carefully open the lid. 3. Strain the cooked eggplant and garlic and add to a food processor along with the parsley, salt, lemon juice and tahini. Pulse to process. Scrape down the sides of the food processor if necessary. 4. Add the olive oil and process until smooth. 5. Serve immediately.

Thai Red Curry Mashed Chickpea

Prep time: 5 minutes | Cook time: 45 minutes | Serves 16

1 cup unsoaked chickpeas

2½ cups water

1 (13.6-ounce / 386-g) can full-fat coconut milk

1 to 2 tablespoon Thai red curry paste

2 tablespoons lime juice

Salt, to taste

1. Add the chickpeas and water to the pressure cooker. 2. Close and lock the pressure cooker lid. Select the Pressure Cook and set the cooking time for 45 minutes on High Pressure. Press Start. Once the timer goes off, perform a natural pressure release for 20 minutes, then release any remaining pressure. Carefully open the lid. 3. Strain the chickpeas and add to a blender along with the coconut milk, curry paste and lime juice. Blend until smooth and season with salt. 4. Serve immediately.

Cauliflower and Tomato Queso

Prep time: 10 minutes | Cook time: 5 minutes | Makes 4 cups

2 cups cauliflower florets

1 cup water

¾ cup thick-cut carrot coins

¼ cup raw cashews

¼ cup nutritional yeast

1 (10-ounce / 284-g) can diced tomatoes with green chiles

½ teaspoon smoked paprika

½ teaspoon salt

¼ teaspoon chili powder

¼ teaspoon jalapeño powder

⅛ teaspoon mustard powder

2 tablespoons minced red onion

½ cup chopped bell pepper

¼ cup minced cilantro

1. Drain the canned tomatoes and reserve the liquid. Set aside. 2. Add the cauliflower, water, carrots and cashews to the pressure cooker. 3. Close and lock the pressure cooker lid. Select the Pressure Cook and set the cooking time for 5 minutes on High Pressure. Press Start. When the timer goes off, do a quick pressure release. Carefully open the lid. 4. Pour the cooked mixture into a strainer over the sink and drain the extra water. 5. In a blender, put the drained mixture along with the nutritional yeast, liquid drained from the canned tomatoes, smoked paprika, salt, chili powder, jalapeño powder and mustard powder. Blend until smooth. 6. Transfer the blender contents into a mixing bowl and stir in the tomatoes and green chiles, bell pepper, minced onion and cilantro. 7. Serve at room temperature or warm.

Chinese Sesame Baby Carrots

Prep time: 10 minutes | Cook time: 2 minutes | Serves 2

½ pound (227 g) baby carrots, trimmed and scrubbed

¼ cup orange juice

½ cup water

1 tablespoon raisins

½ tablespoon soy sauce

1 tablespoon Shaoxing wine

½ teaspoon garlic powder

½ teaspoon shallot powder

½ teaspoon mustard powder

¼ teaspoon cumin seeds

1 teaspoon vegan butter, at room temperature

1 tablespoon toasted sesame seeds

1. Place all the ingredients, except for the sesame seeds, into the pressure cooker. 2. Close and lock the pressure cooker lid. Select the Pressure Cook and set the cooking time for 2 minutes on High Pressure. Press Start. When the timer goes off, do a quick pressure release. Carefully open the lid. 3. Serve topped with the sesame seeds.

Potato French Fries

Prep time: 10 minutes | Cook time: 23 minutes | Serves 2 to 4

2 large russet potatoes, scrubbed

1 tablespoon avocado oil or extra-virgin olive oil

1 teaspoon dried dill

1 teaspoon dried chives

1 teaspoon dried parsley

1 teaspoon cayenne pepper

2 tablespoons chickpea, soy, buckwheat, or millet flour

1. Cut the potatoes into ¼-inch slices, then cut the slices into ¼-inch strips. Transfer the fries to a large bowl and cover them in 3 to 4 cups water. Soak the fries for 20 minutes. Drain, rinse, and pat dry. 2. Return the potatoes to the bowl. Add the avocado oil, dill, chives, parsley, cayenne, and flour. Toss until well coated. 3. Transfer the coated potatoes to the air fryer basket. Close and lock the air fryer lid. Select Bake, set temperature to 390°F (199°C), and set time to 20 minutes. Press Start. Shake halfway through the cooking time.

Cauliflower Bites

Prep time: 10 minutes | Cook time: 19 minutes | Makes 3 cups

2 tablespoons vegan butter , melted

2 tablespoons hot sauce

1 large head of cauliflower, trimmed and chopped

1 cup panko bread crumbs

1. In a large bowl, combine the butter and hot sauce. Add the cauliflower and toss well to coat. 2. Place the cauliflower in the fryer basket and cook until slightly golden brown, about 12 minutes. 3. Remove the cauliflower from the fryer basket. In a clean large bowl, combine the cauliflower and bread crumbs. Toss gently to coat. 4. Place the cauliflower in the fryer basket. Close and lock the air fryer lid. Select Air Fry, set temperature to 360°F (182°C), and set time to 5 to 7 minutes. Press Start. It will bw done until the bread crumbs are golden brown. 5. Transfer the cauliflower to a platter and serve immediately.

Rice Cereal with Dill

Prep time: 5 minutes | Cook time: 7 minutes | Serves 8

4 cups crispy rice cereal

¼ teaspoon salt

2 teaspoons dill

3 tablespoons grated Parmesan-style topping

1 tablespoon soy sauce

1. In a medium bowl, stir all ingredients together to coat well. 2. Pour into the air fryer baking pan. Place into the air fryer basket 3. Close and lock the air fryer lid. Select Bake, set temperature to 360°F (182°C), and set time to 5 minutes. Press Start. 4. Stir and cook for 2 more minutes.

Banana with Peanut

Prep time: 10 minutes | Cook time: 5 minutes | Serves 4 to 6

½ cup crushed cornflakes

½ cup finely chopped peanuts

¼ cup potato starch

¼ cup maple syrup

2 firm bananas

Oil for misting or cooking spray

1. In a shallow dish, mix together the cornflake crumbs and peanuts. 2. In another shallow dish, place the potato starch. 3. Into a third shallow dish, pour the syrup. 4. Cut the bananas in half crosswise. Cut each half in quarters lengthwise so that you have 16 "sticks." 5. Dip the banana sticks in potato starch and tap to shake off excess. 6. Dip the bananas in the syrup, roll in the crumb mixture, and spray with oil or cooking spray. 7. Place the banana sticks in the air fryer basket in a single layer. If need be, you can stack a few crosswise, but don't overcrowd the basket or they won't brown well. 8. Close and lock the air fryer lid. Select Air Fry, set temperature to 390°F (199°C), and set time to 4 to 5 minutes. Press Start. It will be done until golden brown and crispy. 9. Repeat steps 8 and 9 to cook the remaining bananas.

Pasta Chips

Prep time: 7 minutes | Cook time: 10 minutes | Serves 4

2 cups dry whole wheat bow tie pasta (use brown rice pasta)

1 tablespoon olive oil (or use aquafaba)

1 tablespoon nutritional yeast

1½ teaspoons Italia seasoning blend

½ teaspoon salt

1. Cook the pasta according to your package directions with the important exception of only cooking it for half the time listed, then drain the pasta well. 2. Toss the drained pasta with the olive oil (or aquafaba), nutritional yeast, Italian seasoning blend and salt. 3. Place the mixture in your air fryer basket. You may need to work in batches. Close and lock the air fryer lid. Select Air Fry, set temperature to 390°F (199°C), and set time to 5 minutes. Press Start. Shake the basket and cook 3 to 5 minutes more or until crunchy.

Cashews with Molasses

Prep time: 5 minutes | Cook time: 10 minutes | Makes 3 cups

3 cups raw cashews (I recommend whole cashews for this recipe, but you can use halves and pieces. Just reduce the baking time by a few minutes.)

2 teaspoons salt

3 tablespoons liquid smoke

2 tablespoons blackstrap molasses

1. In a large bowl, toss together all the ingredients, making sure to coat the cashews really well (and really evenly!). 2. Pour the cashews into your air fryer basket. Close and lock the air fryer lid. Select Bake, set temperature to 350°F (177°C), and set time to 8 to 10 minutes. Press Start. Shake every 2 minutes to make sure they cook evenly and to check for doneness. 3. During the last 2

minutes, you should shake and check every minute to avoid burning. The line between done and burned can be thin with this recipe. 4. Let them cool to room temperature—about 10 to 15 minutes—then transfer to an airtight storage container and they should keep at least 3 days.

Chickpeas with Salt

Prep time: 5 minutes | Cook time: 15 minutes | Makes 1 cup

1 (15-ounces / 425-g) can chickpeas, drained

2 teaspoons tex-mex seasoning

¼ teaspoon salt

1 tablespoon olive oil

1. Drain the chickpeas and spread them in a single layer on a couple of paper towels. 2. Cover with another paper towel. Press gently and roll to remove extra moisture. Don't press too hard or you'll crush the chickpeas. 3. Place chickpeas in a medium bowl and sprinkle with seasoning. Stir to coat well. 4. Add the oil and stir again to distribute evenly. Place into the air fryer basket. 5. Close and lock the air fryer lid. Select Air Fry, set temperature to 390°F (199°C), and set time to 12 to 15 minutes. Press Start. Shake the basket about halfway through the cooking time. 6. Cool completely and store in an airtight container.

Radish Chips

Prep time: 20 minutes | Cook time: 18 minutes | Serves 8

8 large radishes

1 tablespoon olive oil

½ teaspoon sea salt

1 teaspoon curry powder

1. Scrub the radishes and trim off the stem and root ends. 2. Using a sharp knife or mandoline, slice the radishes into thin rounds, about ⅛ inch thick. Pat the radish slices dry with a paper towel. 3. Put the radishes into the air fryer basket

and drizzle with the oil; toss to coat. Sprinkle with the salt and toss again. 4. Place the basket in the air fryer basket. Close and lock the air fryer lid. Select Air Fry, set temperature to 400°F (204°C), and set time to 14 to 18 minutes. Press Start. Toss once during cooking time, until the radish chips are crisp and light golden brown. Remove the basket; sprinkle the chips with the curry powder and toss. 5. Serve immediately or let cool and store in an airtight container at room temperature for up to 3 days.

Panko Artichoke Balls

Prep time: 26 minutes | Cook time: 10 minutes | Serves 15 balls

1 (14-ounce / 397-g) can artichoke hearts, drained

1 cup panko bread crumbs

1 tablespoon extra-virgin olive oil

1 teaspoon vegan Worcestershire sauce

2 tablespoons grated Parmesan-style topping

1 cup nut milk of choice

1 tablespoon thinly sliced green onions

1. Using your hands, smash all ingredients together to make a stiff mixture. 2. Shape 1 tablespoon at a time into a smooth, cohesive ball. 3. Place the artichoke balls in the air fryer, close together but not touching. 4. Close and lock the air fryer lid. Select Air Fry, set temperature to 390°F (199°C), and set time to 10 minutes. Press Start. Serve warm or at room temperature.

Chapter 3 Beans and Grains

Almond Green Beans

Prep time: 5 minutes | Cook time: 5 minutes | Serves 4

1 teaspoon sesame oil

4 cloves garlic, thinly sliced

1 pound (454 g) green beans, cut into ½-inch pieces

¼ cup water

¼ teaspoon sea salt

¼ cup almond slivers

1. In the pressure cooker, heat the oil on Sauté mode. 2. Add the garlic and sauté until soft, about 2 minutes. 3. Add the green beans and water. 4. Close and lock the pressure cooker lid. Select the Pressure Cook and set cooking time for 1 minute on High Pressure. Press Start. 5. When timer beeps, use a quick pressure release. 6. Remove the lid, stir in the salt. Add the almond slivers, toss, and serve.

Hummus

Prep time: 5 minutes | Cook time: 20 minutes | Serves 4

1 cup dried chickpeas, soaked in water overnight, rinsed and drained

1 tablespoon sesame oil

½ cup diced yellow onion

4 cloves garlic, minced

½ to 1 teaspoon sea salt

¼ cup tahini

¼ cup lemon juice

1. In the pressure cooker, heat the oil on Sauté mode. 2. Add the onion and garlic and sauté for 3 minutes until the onion is translucent. 3. Add the chickpeas and pour in enough water to cover about 1-inch. 4. Close and lock the pressure cooker lid. Select the Pressure Cook and set cooking time for 14 minutes on High Pressure. Press Start. 5. When timer beeps, use a natural pressure release for 5 minutes, then release any remaining pressure. 6. Remove the lid and stir in the salt. Drain the chickpeas, reserving the cooking broth. 7. Add the chickpeas, tahini, and lemon juice to a food processor. Pulse to a creamy texture. Serve immediately.

Indian Cumin Rice

Prep time: 4 minutes | Cook time: 8 minutes | Serves 4 to 6

1 tablespoon olive oil

2 teaspoons cumin seeds

½ teaspoon ground cardamom

2 cups basmati rice, rinsed well, drained, and dried

2½ cups water

1 teaspoon salt

1. Select Sauté and heat the olive oil until shimmering. 2. Add the cumin seeds and cardamom and cook for about 1 minute until fragrant, stirring frequently. 3. Stir in the rice, water, and salt. 4. Close and lock the pressure cooker lid. Select the Pressure Cook and set the cooking time for 6 minutes at High Pressure. Press Start. 5. Once cooking is complete, do a natural pressure release for 10 minutes, then release any remaining pressure. Carefully open the lid. 6. Fluff the rice and serve warm.

Creamy Jasmine Rice

Prep time: 5 minutes | Cook time: 4 minutes | Serves 4 to 6

2 cups jasmine rice, rinsed and drained

½ cup water

1 (14-ounce / 397-g) can coconut milk

¼ teaspoon sea salt, plus more as needed

1. Combine the rice, water, coconut milk, and salt into the pressure cooker. 2. Close and lock the pressure cooker lid. Select the Pressure Cook and set the cooking time for 4 minutes at High Pressure. Press Start. 3. Once cooking is complete, do a natural pressure release for 10 minutes, then release any remaining pressure. Carefully open the lid. 4. Fluff the rice and taste and season with more salt, as needed.

Creamy Pumpkin Risotto

Prep time: 5 minutes | Cook time: 15 minutes | Serves 4 to 6

2 ounces (57 g) extra virgin olive oil

2 cloves garlic, minced

1 small yellow onion, chopped

4 cups vegetable stock

2 cups Arborio rice

¾ cup pumpkin purée

1 teaspoon chopped thyme

½ teaspoon nutmeg

½ teaspoon cinnamon

½ teaspoon grated ginger

½ cup coconut cream

Salt, to taste

1. Select Sauté and heat the olive oil. 2. Add the garlic and onion, stirring, and

sauté for 1 to 2 minutes until fragrant. 3. Add the remaining ingredients except the coconut cream and salt to the pressure cooker and stir to combine. 4. Close and lock the pressure cooker lid. Select the Pressure Cook and set the cooking time for 10 minutes at High Pressure. Press Start. 5. When the timer beeps, perform a quick pressure release. Carefully remove the lid. 6. Stir in the coconut cream and season to taste with salt. Serve warm.

Beans with Tomato Sauce

Prep time: 6 minutes | Cook time: 8 minutes | Serves 2

1½ cups cooked or canned butter beans or great Northern beans, rinsed and drained

1 teaspoon extra-virgin olive oil or canola oil

1 small onion, cut into ⅛-inch thick half-moon slices

1 clove garlic, minced

1 (8-ounce / 227-g) can tomato sauce

1 tablespoon coarsely chopped fresh parsley

½ teaspoon dried oregano

½ teaspoon vegan chicken bouillon granules or salt (optional)

¼ teaspoon freshly ground black pepper

1. Place the beans in an air fryer–safe casserole dish or pan. 2. Heat the oil in a medium saucepan on medium-high heat. Add the onion and garlic and sauté for 5 minutes. Add the tomato sauce, parsley, oregano, and bouillon granules. Bring the mixture to a boil, cover the saucepan, reduce the heat to low, and simmer for 3 minutes. 3. Pour the tomato mixture over the beans and mix well. Sprinkle the pepper over the beans. Place the beans in the air fryer basket. 4. Close and lock the air fryer lid. Select Bake, set temperature to 360°F (182°C), and set time to 8 minutes. Press Start. 5. Serve warm.

Bean and Corn Taco Bowls

Prep time: 15 minutes | Cook time: 9 minutes | Serves 4

2 (10-ounces / 283-g) packages frozen cooked brown rice

1 tablespoon olive oil

1 onion, chopped

3 garlic cloves, minced

1 (15-ounces / 425-g) can pinto beans, drained and rinsed

1 cup frozen corn kernels

2/3 cup mild salsa, divided

1/3 cup sour cream

2 tablespoons freshly squeezed lime juice

1 1/3 cups grated vegan Pepper Jack cheese

1. Prepare the rice as directed on the package and set aside. 2. In a 6-inch metal bowl, drizzle the olive oil over the onion and garlic and toss to combine. 3. Put the bowl into the air fryer basket. Close and lock the air fryer lid. Select Bake, set temperature to 375°F (191°C), and set time to 3 to 4 minutes. Press Start. It will be done until the vegetables are tender. 4. Remove the basket from the cooker and add the beans, corn, and 1/3 cup of salsa to the bowl; stir to combine. Return the basket to the cooker. Bake for another 4 to 5 minutes or until the ingredients are hot. 5. Meanwhile, combine the remaining 1/3 cup of salsa, sour cream, and lime juice in a small bowl until well mixed. 6. Divide the rice equally among four bowls. Divide the bean mixture on top. Drizzle with the sour cream mixture and sprinkle with the cheese. Serve.

Bean Rice Stuffed Bell Peppers

Prep time: 20 minutes | Cook time: 20 minutes | Serves 4

4 large red bell peppers

1 (10-ounces / 283-g) package frozen cooked brown rice, thawed

1 (15-ounces / 425-g) can black beans, rinsed and drained

1 cup frozen corn kernels, thawed

1 cup shredded vegan Muenster cheese, divided

1/2 cup salsa

3 scallions, chopped

2 teaspoons chili powder

1/2 teaspoon ground cumin

½ teaspoon sea salt

¼ cup grated vegan Parmesan cheese

1. Rinse the peppers and dry them. Cut off the tops and discard them. Remove the membranes and seeds, being careful to not pierce the pepper sides or bottom. 2. In a large bowl, combine the rice, black beans, corn, ½ cup of Muenster cheese, salsa, scallions, chili powder, cumin, and salt and mix well. Stuff the peppers with this mixture, overstuffing them a bit as the filling will shrink as it cooks. 3. Put the peppers in the air fryer basket, nestling them against one another so they stay upright. 4. Close and lock the air fryer lid. Select Bake, set temperature to 350°F (177°C), and set time to 10 minutes. Press Start. 5. Top with the remaining ½ cup of Muenster cheese and the Parmesan cheese and continue baking for 5 to 10 minutes or until the peppers are softened, the filling is hot, and the cheese is melted. Serve.

Pineapple Brown Rice Bake

Prep time: 4 minutes | Cook time: 6 to 8 minutes | Serves 2 to 4

1 teaspoon sesame oil

⅓ cup chopped onion

⅓ cup chopped bell pepper

2 cups cooked brown rice

1 (8-ounces / 227-g) can crushed pineapple, drained

½ teaspoon salt

1. In the baking pan, add the oil, onion, and bell pepper. Place the pan into air fryer basket. Close and lock the air fryer lid. Select Bake, set temperature to 390°F (199°C), and set time to 1 minute. Press Start. Open the lid and stir. 2. Bake the veggie mixture for 3 to 4 more minutes or just until the vegetables become tender. 3. Transfer the vegetables to a bowl and add the rice, pineapple, and salt, stirring until well mixed. 4. Pour the mixture back into the baking pan in the air fryer basket and bake at 390°F (199°C) for 2 to 3 minutes, until everything heats through.

Chapter 4 Soups and Stews

Paprika Carrot Soup

Prep time: 10 minutes | Cook time: 4 minutes | Serves 2 to 3

7 carrots, chopped

1¼ cups vegetable stock

1 (1-inch) piece fresh ginger, peeled and chopped

½ sweet onion, chopped

½ teaspoon sweet paprika

½ teaspoon salt, plus more as needed

Freshly ground black pepper, to taste

Fresh herbs, for garnish (optional)

1. In the pressure cooker, combine the carrots, stock, ginger, onion, paprika, and salt. Season to taste with pepper. 2. Close and lock the pressure cooker lid. Select the Pressure Cook and set the cooking time for 4 minutes at High Pressure. Press Start. 3. Once cooking is complete, do a natural pressure release for 5 minutes, then release any remaining pressure. Carefully open the lid. 4. Using an immersion blender, blend the soup until completely smooth. Taste and season with more salt and pepper, as needed. If desired, serve garnished with fresh herbs.

Easy Creamy Tomato Basil Soup

Prep time: 5 minutes | Cook time: 10 minutes | Serves 4 to 6

2 tablespoons vegan butter

1 small sweet onion, chopped

2 garlic cloves, minced

1 celery stalk, chopped

1 large carrot, chopped

3 cups vegetable stock

3 pounds (1.4 kg) tomatoes, quartered

¼ cup nutritional yeast

¼ cup chopped fresh basil, plus more for garnish

Salt, to taste

Freshly ground black pepper, to taste

½ to 1 cup coconut milk

1. Select Sauté and melt the butter. 2. Add the onion and garlic and sauté for 3 to 4 minutes, stirring frequently. Add the celery and carrot and cook for another 1 to 2 minutes, stirring frequently. Pour in the stock. 3. Add the tomatoes, yeast, ¼

cup of basil, and a pinch of salt. Stir well. 4. Close and lock the pressure cooker lid. Select the Pressure Cook and set the cooking time for 5 minutes at High Pressure. Press Start. 5. Once cooking is complete, do a natural pressure release for 8 minutes, then release any remaining pressure. Carefully open the lid. 6. Using an immersion blender, blend the soup to your preferred consistency. Whisk in the milk. Taste and season with more salt and pepper, if desired. Garnish with the fresh basil and serve.

Leek and Potato Soup

Prep time: 5 minutes | Cook time: 10 minutes | Serves 4

3 tablespoons vegan butter

2 large leeks, white and very light green parts only, cleaned well and chopped

2 garlic cloves, minced

4 cups vegetable stock

1 pound (454 g) Yukon Gold potatoes, cubed

1 bay leaf

½ teaspoon salt, plus more as needed

⅓ cup extra-virgin olive oil

⅔ cup soy milk

Freshly ground white pepper, to taste

1. Select Sauté and melt the butter. 2. Add the leeks and sauté for about 2 to 3 minutes until tender, stirring occasionally. 3. Add the garlic and cook for 30 to 45 seconds more, stirring frequently, until fragrant. 4. Pour in the stock and add the potatoes, bay leaf, and salt. Stir to mix well. 5. Close and lock the pressure cooker lid. Select the Pressure Cook and set the cooking time for 5 minutes at High Pressure. Press Start. 6. Once cooking is complete, do a natural pressure release for 15 minutes, then release any remaining pressure. 7. In a blender, combine the olive oil and soy milk. Blend until completely mixed. This is an easy dairy-free substitute for heavy cream. 8. Carefully open the lid, remove and discard the bay leaf. Whisk in the "cream." Using an immersion blender, purée the soup until smooth. 9. Taste and season with more salt and pepper, as needed. Serve immediately.

Coconut Curry Lentil and Kale Soup

Prep time: 10 minutes | Cook time: 15 minutes | Serves 4

1 tablespoon coconut oil	2 cups vegetable broth
2 cloves garlic, minced	2 cups unsweetened coconut milk
1 tablespoon fresh grated ginger	1½ cup red lentils, rinsed and drained
1 cup sliced sweet yellow onion	½ cup chopped cashews
2 cups chopped kale	1 tablespoon chopped fresh lemongrass (optional)
2 tablespoons red curry paste	

1. Select Sauté and melt the coconut oil. 2. Add the garlic, ginger, onion and kale. Sauté for 3 minutes, stirring occasionally. 3. Stir in the red curry paste and sauté for 1 to 2 minutes more. 4. Add the vegetable broth, coconut milk, and lentils and stir well. 5. Close and lock the pressure cooker lid. Select the Pressure Cook and set the cooking time for 10 minutes at High Pressure. Press Start. 6. Once cooking is complete, do a quick pressure release. Carefully open the lid. 7. Ladle the soup into serving bowls. Serve garnished with the cashews and lemongrass (if desired).

Easy Swiss Chard Stem Soup

Prep time: 3 minutes | Cook time: 4 minutes | Serves 6

8 cups diced Swiss Chard stems	1½ cups vegetable stock
3 leeks, chopped	1 cup coconut milk
1 potato, peeled and diced	Salt and pepper, to taste
1 celeriac, peeled and diced	

1. Combine all the ingredients into the pressure cooker. 2. Close and lock the pressure cooker lid. Select the Pressure Cook and set the cooking time for 4 minutes at High Pressure. Press Start. 3. When the timer beeps, perform a natural pressure release for 8 minutes, then release any remaining pressure. Carefully remove the lid. Serve warm.

Dill Celery Soup

Prep time: 10 minutes | Cook time: 30 minutes | Serves 8

2 bunches celery, diced

2 sweet yellow onions, diced

4 cups vegetable broth

2 cups coconut milk

1 teaspoon dill

2 pinches of sea salt

1. Combine all the ingredients into the pressure cooker. 2. Close and lock the pressure cooker lid. Select the Pressure Cook mode and set the cooking time for 30 minutes at High Pressure. Press Start. 3. Once cooking is complete, do a natural pressure release for 10 minutes, then release any remaining pressure. Carefully open the lid. 4. Use an immersion blender to blend the soup into a smooth mixture. 5. Serve hot.

Mushroom Barley Soup

Prep time: 5 minutes | Cook time: 30 minutes | Serves 6

1 teaspoon vegetable oil

2 cloves garlic, minced

½ cup diced onion

3 stalks celery, chopped

2 carrots, diced

2 large portobello mushrooms, sliced lengthwise, then sliced again

1 tomato, diced

4 cups water

3 cups vegetable broth

¾ cup pearl barley, rinsed and drained

2 sprigs fresh thyme

½ to 1 teaspoon salt

Ground black pepper, to taste

1. Press the Sauté button on the pressure cooker and heat the oil. 2. Add the garlic and onion and sauté for 2 to 3 minutes, until the onion is tender. 3. Add the celery and carrot and sauté for an additional 3 to 5 minutes, until the celery is softened. 4. Add the mushrooms, tomato, barley, broth, water, and thyme, stirring well. 6. Close and lock the pressure cooker lid. Select the Pressure Cook and set the cooking time for 20 minutes at High Pressure. Press Start. 7. Once cooking is complete, do a natural pressure release for 10 minutes, then release any remaining pressure. Carefully open the lid and stir in the salt. 8. Season to taste with black pepper and serve.

Coconut Chickpea and Mushroom Stew

Prep time: 10 minutes | Cook time: 3 minutes | Serves 4

3 cups cooked chickpeas (from 1 cup dried)

8 ounces (227 g) mushrooms, sliced (about 3 cups)

1 red bell pepper, deseeded and chopped

2 tablespoons tamari

1 teaspoon Thai chili paste

1 (13.5-ounce / 383-g) can coconut milk

1 teaspoon ground ginger

Salt, to taste

1. In the pressure cooker, combine the chickpeas, mushrooms, red bell pepper, tamari, chili paste, coconut milk, and ginger. 2. Close and lock the pressure cooker lid, then select the Pressure Cook and set cooking time for 3 minutes on High Pressure. Press Start. 3. Once the cook time is complete, let the pressure release naturally for about 20 minutes, then release any remaining pressure. Open the lid. 4. Season with salt before serving.

Peas and Potato Stew

Prep time: 5 minutes | Cook time: 15 minutes | Serves 5

3 potatoes, peeled, chopped

2 carrots, chopped

1 cup green peas, frozen

1 tablespoon tomato paste

2 cups water

1 teaspoon salt

1 teaspoon cayenne pepper

1. Place the potatoes, carrots, and green peas into the pressure cooker. 2. In a bowl, combine the tomato paste, water, salt, and cayenne pepper. 3. Whisk until it gets a light red color and then pour the mixture into the pressure cooker. 4. Close and lock the pressure cooker lid. Select the Pressure Cook and set cooking time for 10 minutes on High Pressure. Press Start. 5. When timer beeps, use a natural pressure release for 5 minutes, then release any remaining pressure. Open the lid. 6. Serve immediately.

Chapter 5 Vegetables and Sides

Cauliflower and Millet Mash

Prep time: 10 minutes | Cook time: 13 minutes | Serves 6 to 8

1½ tablespoons olive oil

2 medium leeks, dark green tops discarded, rinsed, trimmed and diced

3 garlic cloves, minced

1 cup millet

2¼ cups low-sodium vegetable broth

1 medium cauliflower, cut into florets

2 teaspoons kosher salt, plus more to taste

Freshly cracked black pepper, to taste

2 to 3 tablespoons tahini

1 teaspoon apple cider vinegar

½ cup chopped fresh Italian flat-leaf parsley

1. Select the Sauté setting on the pressure cooker and heat the olive oil. Add the leeks. Cook until the leeks are tender, 2 to 3 minutes. Add the garlic and cook for 1 minute, stirring frequently to prevent burning. 2. Add the millet and toss for 30 to 60 seconds to coat the grains. Pour in the vegetable broth, followed by the cauliflower, salt, and pepper to taste. 3. Close and lock the pressure cooker lid. Select the Pressure Cook and set the cooking time for 10 minutes on High Pressure. Press Start. Once the timer goes off, perform a natural pressure release for 10 minutes, then release any remaining pressure. Carefully open the lid. 4. Stir to combine the ingredients. Using an immersion blender, carefully blend the millet-cauliflower mixture until the texture is similar to thick mashed potatoes. 5. Drizzle in 2 tablespoons of the tahini and the vinegar, stir to incorporate, and taste for seasonings. Add a third tablespoon of the tahini and a bit more salt as needed. 6. Top with chopped parsley and serve warm.

Easy Rosemary Red Potatoes

Prep time: 5 minutes | Cook time: 10 minutes | Serves 4

4 cups cubed red potatoes

1 cup water

1 tablespoon olive oil

1 tablespoon fresh rosemary

1 teaspoon granulated garlic

1 teaspoon coarse ground black pepper

½ teaspoon salt

1. Pour the water and insert a steamer basket into the pressure cooker. Place the cubed potatoes in the basket. 2. Close and lock the pressure cooker lid. Select the Steam mode and set the cooking time for 8 minutes on High Pressure. Press Start. When the timer goes off, do a quick pressure release. Carefully open the lid. 3. While the potatoes are steaming, preheat the broiler of your oven and line a baking sheet with aluminum foil. 4. When the timer goes off, do a quick pressure release. Carefully open the lid. Remove the potatoes. Spread the steamed potatoes out on the baking sheet. 5. Drizzle the potatoes with the olive oil and season them with the fresh rosemary, granulated garlic, salt and coarse ground black pepper. Toss gently, taking care to smash the steamed potatoes. 6. Place the baking sheet under the broiler for 2 minutes. 7. Remove and serve immediately.

Garlicky Steamed Broccoli

Prep time: 5 minutes | Cook time: 10 minutes | Serves 6

6 cups broccoli florets

2 tablespoons peanut oil

1 cup water

2 tablespoons Chinese rice wine

½ garlic cloves, minced

Sea salt, to taste

1. Pour the water and insert the trivet into the pressure cooker. Arrange the broccoli florets over the trivet. 2. Close and lock the pressure cooker lid. Select the Pressure Cook and set the cooking time for 5 minutes on High Pressure. Press Start. Once the timer goes off, perform a natural pressure release for 5 minutes, then release any remaining pressure. Carefully open the lid. 3. Strain the florets and return them back to the pot. Add the remaining ingredients to the broccoli. 4. Select the Sauté mode and sauté for 5 minutes. 5. Serve.

Garlicky White Beets

Prep time: 10 minutes | Cook time: 13 minutes | Serves 4

6 whole white beets

4 cups water

2 teaspoons salt

2 tablespoons olive oil

4 cloves garlic, minced

2 tablespoons lime juice

1. Separate the white part of the beets from the green ones. Wash and rinse. 2. Cut the white parts into cubes and add them to the pressure cooker along with water. 3. Close and lock the pressure cooker lid. Select the Pressure Cook and set the cooking time for 10 minutes on High Pressure. Press Start. Once the timer goes off, perform a natural pressure release for 15 minutes, then release any remaining pressure. Carefully open the lid. 4. Add the green parts of the beets to the pressure cooker and let it stay for 5 minutes. Strain the beets and set them aside. 5. Select the Sauté mode. Add the oil and garlic to the pressure cooker and sauté for 2 minutes. 6. Return the beets to the cooker and sauté for 1 minute.7. Drizzle with the lime juice and salt. Serve.

Rosemary Carrots

Prep time: 10 minutes | Cook time: 15 minutes | Serves 4

2½ pounds (1.1 kg) carrots, sliced

3 tablespoons avocado oil

Salt and black pepper, to taste

1 cup veggie stock

1 teaspoon garam masala

½ teaspoon sweet chili powder

1 teaspoon dried rosemary

1. Press the Sauté button on the pressure cooker and heat the oil. Add the carrots and sauté for 5 minutes. Stir in the remaining ingredients. 2. Close and lock the pressure cooker lid. Select the Pressure Cook and set the cooking time for 10 minutes on High Pressure. Press Start. Once the timer goes off, perform a natural pressure release for 10 minutes, then release any remaining pressure. Carefully open the lid. 3. Divide the mix between plates and serve as a side dish.

Garlicky Boiled Bok Choy

Prep time: 5 minutes | Cook time: 7 minutes | Serves 2

1 garlic clove, smashed

1 bunch bok choy, trimmed

1 cup water

Salt and pepper, to taste

1. Add the water, garlic and bok choy to the pressure cooker. 2. Close and lock the pressure cooker lid. Select the Pressure Cook and set the cooking time for 7 minutes on High Pressure. Press Start. When the timer goes off, do a quick pressure release. Carefully open the lid. 3. Strain the cooked bok choy and transfer it to a platter. 4. Sprinkle some salt and pepper on top. 5. Serve.

Coconut Cauliflower Mash

Prep time: 10 minutes | Cook time: 8 minutes | Serves 4

1 pound (454 g) cauliflower florets

1 teaspoon Italian seasoning

1 teaspoon dried sage

Salt and black pepper, to taste

2 spring onions, chopped

¼ cup coconut cream

½ cup vegetable stock

1. In your pressure cooker, mix the cauliflower with the stock, salt, pepper, Italian seasoning and the sage. 2, Close and lock the pressure cooker lid. Select the Pressure Cook and set the cooking time for 8 minutes on High Pressure. Press Start. Once the timer goes off, perform a natural pressure release for 10 minutes, then release any remaining pressure. Carefully open the lid. 3. Mash the mix with a potato masher, add the remaining ingredients, whisk well, divide between plates and serve as a side dish.

Citrus Brussels Sprouts

Prep time: 10 minutes | Cook time: 8 minutes | Serves 6

1½ pounds (680 g) Brussels sprouts, halved

Pinch of salt and black pepper

¼ cup orange juice

1 teaspoon grated orange zest

1 teaspoon grated lime zest

1 tablespoon olive oil

1. Add all the ingredients to the pressure cooker and stir to combine. 2. Close and lock the pressure cooker lid. Select the Pressure Cook and set the cooking time for

8 minutes on High Pressure. Press Start. Once the timer goes off, perform a natural pressure release for 10 minutes, then release any remaining pressure. Carefully open the lid. 3. Divide the mix between plates and serve.

Avocado Fries

Prep time: 6 minutes | Cook time: 10 minutes | Serves 4

½ cup panko bread crumbs (use gluten-free panko)

½ teaspoon salt

Aquafaba from 1 (15-ounce / 425-g) can white beans or garbanzo beans (I haven't tried with other bean liquids, but it should work just fine.)

1 Haas avocado, peeled, pitted and sliced

1. In a shallow bowl, toss together the panko and salt. Pour the aquafaba into another shallow bowl. 2. Dredge the avocado slices in the aquafaba and then in the panko, getting a nice, even coating. Arrange the slices in a single layer in your air fryer basket. The single layer is important. No overlapping, please! 3. Close and lock the air fryer lid. Select Air Fry, set temperature to 390°F (199°C), and set time to 10 minutes. Press Start. Shake well after 5 minutes. 4. Serve immediately with your favorite dipping sauce! 5. You want your avocado fries to be lightly browned and crunchy. When you do that shake after 5 minutes, take a look at the progress. They should be beginning to brown, and the panko shouldn't fall off when you shake. If your breading isn't solid after 5 minutes, keep checking once a minute before doing vigorous shaking.

Parsnip with Cinnamon

Prep time: 10 minutes | Cook time: 15 minutes | Serves 2 to 4

2 medium parsnips, trimmed and well washed

1 teaspoon avocado oil or canola oil

1 teaspoon ground cinnamon

½ teaspoon ground cumin

½ teaspoon paprika

½ teaspoon ground coriander

½ teaspoon sea salt

¼ teaspoon black pepper

½ teaspoon cornstarch

1 tablespoon spelt flour or brown rice flour

1. Trim the tops and bottoms of the parsnips. Slice in half lengthwise. Halve or quarter the thick parts lengthwise, until all parsnip pieces are roughly the same size. 2. Transfer them to a large bowl. Add the oil, cinnamon, cumin, paprika, coriander, salt, and pepper. 3. In a small bowl, combine the cornstarch and flour. Sprinkle the cornstarch mixture over the parsnips and toss with tongs until well coated, and then place into the air fryer basket 4. Close and lock the air fryer lid. Select Roast, set temperature to 370°F (188°C), and set time to 15 minutes. Press Start. It will be done until golden brown, shaking halfway through the cooking time.

Squash Seeds with Tamari

Prep time: 7 minutes | Cook time: 9 minutes | Serves 1 to 2

¼ to ½ cup acorn or butternut squash seeds (the amount varies by the size of squash)

2 tablespoons low-sodium tamari or low-sodium soy sauce

¼ teaspoon white pepper or freshly ground black pepper

1. Rinse the squash seeds well, removing any strings or bits of squash. Transfer them to a small bowl or measuring cup. Pour the tamari over the seeds and let them marinate for 30 minutes. 2. Drain (but don't rinse) the seeds. 3. Transfer the seeds to the air fryer basket and sprinkle with the white pepper. Close and lock the air fryer lid. Select Bake, set temperature to 390°F (199°C), and set time to 6 minutes. Press Start. Shake halfway through the cooking time. Eat the seeds immediately or store them in an airtight container for 3 days.

Yucca Root

Prep time: 5 minutes | Cook time: 14 minutes | Serves 4

1¼ pounds (567 g) yucca root, peeled

1 tablespoon olive oil

½ teaspoon kosher salt

1. Cut the yucca into equally sized fries. In a large bowl, combine the fries, olive oil, and salt. Toss well to coat. 2. Place the fries in the fryer basket. Close and lock the air fryer lid. Select Bake, set temperature to 350°F (177°C), and set time to 10 to 14 minutes. Press Start. It will be done until golden and crispy, Pause the machine halfway through to shake the basket. 3. Transfer the fries to a platter and serve immediately.

Eggplants with Tahini Sauce

Prep time: 10 minutes | Cook time: 20 minutes | Serves 2

2 small eggplants

4 teaspoons olive oil

Kosher salt, to taste

Freshly ground black pepper, to taste

The Sauce:

¼ cup tahini

2 teaspoons agave nectar

¼ teaspoon ground cumin

1 tablespoon freshly squeezed lemon juice

2 tablespoons water

½ cup pomegranate seeds

2 tablespoons chopped fresh mint

1. In a small bowl, make the tahini sauce by whisking together the tahini, agave, cumin, lemon juice, and water until smooth. (Add a few more drops of water if needed.) Set aside. 2. Cut the eggplants in half lengthwise. Use a paring knife to score the flesh lengthwise and across. (Be careful not to cut all the way through to the skin.) 3. Lay the eggplants on a flat surface and gently press to open. Drizzle olive oil over the flesh and season with salt and pepper. 4. Place the eggplants cut

side up in the fryer basket. Close and lock the air fryer lid. Select Roast, set temperature to 300°F (149°C), and set time to 20 minutes. Press Start. It will be done until tender and caramelized. 5. Transfer the eggplants to a serving platter. Drizzle the tahini sauce over the eggplants. Sprinkle the pomegranate seeds and mint around the platter. Serve immediately.

Mushroom with Sauce

Prep time: 5 minutes | Cook time: 5 minutes | Serves 2 to 4

8 ounces (227 g) sliced white mushrooms

¼ teaspoon garlic powder

1 tablespoon vegan Worcestershire sauce

1. Rinse and drain the mushrooms well. 2. In a large bowl, add the mushrooms and sprinkle them with the garlic powder and vegan Worcestershire sauce. Stir well to distribute evenly. 3. Place the mushrooms in the air fryer basket. Close and lock the air fryer lid. Select Air Fry, set temperature to 390°F (199°C), and set time to 4 to 5 minutes. Press Start. It will be done until the mushrooms become tender.

Zucchini and Squash Ratatouille

Prep time: 20 minutes | Cook time: 20 minutes | Serves 2 to 3

1½ cups diced zucchini (½-inch dice)

1½ cups diced yellow crookneck squash (½-inch dice)

½ cup diced bell peppers (½-inch dice)

½ cup diced onion (½-inch dice)

1 to 3 cloves garlic, minced

1 tablespoon extra-virgin olive oil

1 tablespoon tuscan herb mix

½ teaspoon salt

6 to 8 cherry tomatoes

1. Combine the zucchini, squash, bell pepper, onion, and garlic with the oil, tuscan herb mix, and salt and toss to coat thoroughly. 2. Spoon the veggie mixture into the air fryer baking pan. Place the pan into air fryer basket. 3. Close and lock the air fryer lid. Select Bake, set temperature to 390°F (199°C), and set time to 10 minutes. Press Start. 4. Stir and add the cherry tomatoes. 5. Cook for 10 more minutes and stir before serving.

Green Beans with Sesame

Prep time: 10 minutes | Cook time: 22 minutes | Serves 4

1 pound (454 g) fresh green beans

1 tablespoon sesame oil

½ medium onion, julienned

1 tablespoon sesame seeds

¼ teaspoon crushed red pepper flakes

Oil for misting

1 tablespoon soy sauce

1. Wash the beans and snap off the stem ends. 2. In a large bowl, toss the beans with the sesame oil. 3. Place them in the air fryer basket. Close and lock the air fryer lid. Select Bake, set temperature to 330°F (166°C), and set time to 5 minutes. Press Start. 4. Shake the basket and cook for 5 more minutes. 5. If needed, continue cooking for 2 to 4 minutes, until the beans are as tender as you like. They may shrivel slightly and brown in places. 6. Remove from the basket and set aside. 7. Place the slivered onion in the air fryer baking pan. Stir in the sesame seeds and red pepper and mist with oil. 8. Place the pan into air fryer basket. Close and lock the air fryer lid. Select Bake, set temperature to 330°F (166°C), and set time to 5 minutes. Press Start. 9. Open the lid and stir, and, if needed, cook 2 to 3 more minutes until the onion becomes crisp-tender. 10. Stir the soy sauce into the onions. Pour the onion mixture over the green beans and stir well to combine.

Okra with Paprika

Prep time: 6 minutes | Cook time: 10 minutes | Serves 4

4 cups sliced okra (about 16 ounces / 454 g), fresh or frozen

⅔ cup unsweetened nondairy milk

½ cup cornmeal

¼ cup whole wheat pastry flour (or use gluten-free baking mix)

1 teaspoon Cajun seasoning blend

½ teaspoon garlic powder

½ teaspoon salt

¼ teaspoon paprika

¼ teaspoon cayenne pepper powder (optional)

⅛ teaspoon black pepper

Spray oil for cooking (optional)

1. Add about 1 cup of the okra and all the nondairy milk to a small bowl and mix. 2. In a larger bowl, add the cornmeal, flour, Cajun seasoning, garlic powder, salt, paprika, cayenne (if using) and black pepper. Mix well. 3. Use a slotted spoon and take some of the okra out of the soaking bowl, and drop them into the dry mixture. Shake or stir with a dry fork to get all parts of the okra coated with the dry mixture. 4. Use a dry slotted spoon and transfer the coated pieces of okra to your air fryer basket in a single layer. Repeat until your fryer basket is full. 5. Add the basket full of okra, spritz some oil on top, if using. Close and lock the air fryer lid. Select Air Fry, set temperature to 390°F (199°C), and set time to 5 minutes. Press Start. Shake the basket (or use a wooden spoon if your basket is mesh), spray more oil if desired and cook 5 minutes more. 6. Repeat from the beginning of the instructions until all the okra has been cooked. The size of your air fryer will determine how many cooking rounds you'll need.

Panko Pickles

Prep time: 5 minutes | Cook time: 5 minutes | Serves 8

2 cups dill pickle slices

Batter:

¼ cup whole wheat flour (use gluten-free)

¼ cup finely ground cornmeal

½ teaspoon salt

¾ cup soy milk plus 1 teaspoon apple cider vinegar (use any unsweetened nondairy milk and leave out the vinegar)

2 tablespoons organic cornstarch or tapioca starch

1½ cups whole wheat panko bread crumbs (use gluten-free)

1. Place the pickle slices in a colander over the sink while you make the batter.

Make the Batter

2. Mix the flour, cornmeal and salt together in a small mixing bowl. Add the curdled soy milk (or other nondairy milk) and mix again. 3. Place the starch in a small bowl and the bread crumbs in another. Stab a pickle with a fork, dust it in the starch, then dip it into the batter. Let the excess batter roll off, then place in the panko, turn over and press the bread crumbs on firmly. Place in your air fryer basket. Repeat until all the pickle slices are coated. 4. Close and lock the air fryer lid. Select Air Fry, set temperature to 400°F (204°C), and set time to 5 minutes. Press Start. If they are not quite golden brown, cook 1 or 2 minutes more. Repeat until all the pickles are cooked.

Onion Rings with Aquafaba

Prep time: 8 minutes | Cook time: 7 minutes | Serves 2 to 4

1 large onion, cut into ¼-inch thick slices

1 cup unbleached all-purpose flour

¼ cup chickpea flour

1 teaspoon baking powder

1 teaspoon sea salt

½ cup aquafaba or vegan egg substitute

1 cup soymilk

¾ cup panko bread crumbs

1. Separate the onion slices into rings. 2. Combine the all-purpose flour, chickpea

flour, baking powder, and salt in a small bowl. 3. Dredge the onion slices in the flour mixture until well coated. Set aside. 4. Whisk the aquafaba and milk into the remaining flour mixture. Dip the floured onion rings into the batter to coat. 5. Spread the panko bread crumbs on a plate or shallow dish and dredge the rings into the crumbs, covering well. 6. Place the onion rings into the air fryer in a single layer. Close and lock the air fryer lid. Select Bake, set temperature to 360°F (182°C), and set time to 7 minutes. Press Start. Shake halfway through the cooking time.

Potato Truffle

Prep time: 10 minutes | Cook time: 18 minutes | Serves 4

1½ pounds (680 g) russet potatoes

1 tablespoon olive oil

¼ teaspoon kosher salt

1 teaspoon truffle salt

1. Cut the potatoes into equally sized fries. In a large bowl, combine the fries, olive oil, and kosher salt. Toss well to coat. 2. Place the fries in the fryer basket. Close and lock the air fryer lid. Select , set temperature to 350°F (177°C), and set time to 15 to 18 minutes. Press Start. It will be done until golden and crispy. Pause the machine halfway through to shake the basket. 3. Transfer the fries to a platter and season with the truffle salt before serving.

Dill Carrot

Prep time: 5 minutes | Cook time: 22 minutes | Serves 4

2 cups baby carrots

1 large carrot, peeled and sliced ½ inch thick

1 tablespoon freshly squeezed orange juice

2 teaspoons olive oil

1 teaspoon vegan butter, melted

1 teaspoon dried dill weed

½ teaspoon sea salt

⅛ teaspoon freshly ground black

pepper

1. Pat the carrots dry with paper towels and place them in the air fryer basket. 2. In a small bowl, combine the orange juice, olive oil, butter, dill weed, salt, and pepper and mix well. Drizzle over the carrots and toss to coat. Place the basket in the air fryer. 3. Close and lock the air fryer lid. Select Roast, set temperature to 400°F (204°C), and set time to 10 minutes. Press Start. Shake the basket and roast for another 8 to 12 minutes or until the carrots are tender and glazed. Serve.

Chapter 6 Vegetable Mains

Thyme Sweet Potato Mash

Prep time: 10 minutes | Cook time: 10 minutes | Serves 4

2 cups water

6 cups peeled and cubed sweet potatoes

¼ cup vegan butter

3 cloves garlic, minced

½ teaspoon dried chipotle pepper

½ teaspoon dried thyme

Pinch of salt

Pinch of freshly ground black pepper

1. Pour the water into the pressure cooker and add the sweet potatoes, butter, and garlic. 2. Close and lock the pressure cooker lid. Select the Pressure Cook and set the cooking time for 10 minutes on High Pressure. Press Start. Once the timer goes off, perform a natural pressure release for 10 minutes, then release any remaining pressure. Carefully open the lid. 3. Drain any remaining liquid from the cooker and add the chipotle pepper and thyme. Mash the potatoes using a potato masher or electric mixer. 4. Season with salt and pepper and serve.

Mushroom Risotto with Arborio Rice

Prep time: 5 minutes | Cook time: 18 minutes | Serves 6

1 tablespoon olive oil

½ medium yellow onion, peeled and diced

1 clove garlic, minced	1 tablespoon vegan butter
2 cups Arborio rice	Pinch of salt
6 cups vegetable broth, divided	Pinch of freshly ground black pepper
2 cups chopped assorted mushrooms	

1. Press the Sauté button on the pressure cooker and add the olive oil. Add the onion and sauté until just soft, about 3 minutes. Add the garlic and sauté an additional 30 seconds. Add the rice and sauté 4 minutes or until the rice becomes opaque. 2. Add 5 cups of the vegetable broth to the cooker. 3. Close and lock the pressure cooker lid. Select the Pressure Cook and set the cooking time for 6 minutes on High Pressure. Press Start. When the timer goes off, do a quick pressure release. Carefully open the lid. 4. Press the Sauté button on the cooker and stir in the remaining 1 cup of the broth and the mushrooms. Let the risotto simmer until the liquid is absorbed, about 5 minutes. 5. Add the vegan butter to the risotto and season with salt and pepper just before serving.

Spicy and Sweet Braised Red Cabbage

Prep time: 10 minutes | Cook time: 3 minutes | Makes 7 cups

1 tablespoon olive oil	¼ cup apple cider vinegar
1 medium red cabbage, roughly chopped	1½ tablespoons reduced-sodium tamari
1¼ teaspoons kosher salt, divided	1 tablespoon organic brown sugar
2 large carrots, grated	½ cup dried sour cherries
1 apple, unpeeled and grated	1 teaspoon crushed red pepper flakes
1¼ cups low-sodium vegetable broth	2 teaspoons white sesame seeds

1. Select the Sauté setting on the pressure cooker and let the cooker heat up for a few minutes before adding the olive oil. Once the oil is hot, add the cabbage. Add ½ teaspoon of the kosher salt and cook, stirring occasionally, until the cabbage begins to brown, about 4 minutes. 2. Top the cabbage with the carrots and apple, then pour in the vegetable broth, vinegar, and tamari and add the brown sugar, dried cherries, pepper flakes, and the remaining ¾ teaspoon of the salt. Stir well to combine. 3. Close and lock the pressure cooker lid. Select the Pressure Cook

and set the cooking time for 3 minutes on High Pressure. Press Start. When the timer goes off, do a quick pressure release. Carefully open the lid. 4. Transfer the cabbage to a serving dish and serve garnished with the sesame seeds.

Mashed Root Vegetables

Prep time: 15 minutes | Cook time: 9 to 10 minutes | Serves 8

1 head garlic, roasted

1 cup water

1 tablespoon olive oil

1 medium yellow onion, roughly chopped

1 pound (454 g) carrots, peeled and cut into large cubes

1 pound (454 g) sweet potatoes, peeled and cut into pieces slightly larger than the carrots

1 small head cauliflower, roughly chopped into florets

1 large sprig fresh rosemary

6 sprigs fresh thyme

1¼ teaspoons kosher salt, divided

Freshly cracked black pepper, to taste

⅓ cup low-sodium vegetable broth

2 tablespoons vegan butter

1. Select the Sauté setting and let the cooker heat up for a few minutes before adding the olive oil. Once the oil is hot, add the onion. Cook until the onion is lightly browned, 4 to 5 minutes. 2. Add the carrots, sweet potatoes, cauliflower, rosemary, and thyme. Squeeze the roasted garlic cloves directly into the pressure cooker and season with ¾ teaspoon of the salt and pepper. Pour the vegetable broth on top and stir all the ingredients to combine. 3. Close and lock the pressure cooker lid. Select the Pressure Cook and set the cooking time for 5 minutes on High Pressure. Press Start. When the timer goes off, do a quick pressure release. Carefully open the lid. 4. Add the vegan butter and the remaining ½ teaspoon of the salt. Using an immersion blender, blend all the ingredients together until you have a smooth texture. 5. Serve warm.

Sesame-Garlic Green Beans

Prep time: 5 minutes | Cook time: 5 minutes | Serves 4

5 cups green beans, trimmed

4 cloves garlic, sliced

½ cup vegetable broth

1 tablespoon sesame oil

1 tablespoon toasted sesame seeds

¼ cup chopped red bell pepper

1. Combine the green beans, garlic and vegetable broth into the pressure cooker. 2. Close and lock the pressure cooker lid. Select the Pressure Cook and set the cooking time for 5 minutes on High Pressure. Press Start. When the timer goes off, do a quick pressure release. Carefully open the lid. 3. Remove the green beans and drain them thoroughly, reserving the sliced garlic as you do so. 4. Transfer the green beans to a bowl, along with the reserved garlic. Add the sesame oil and the toasted sesame seeds. Toss to coat. 5. Garnish the dish with chopped red bell pepper before serving.

Classic Brazilian Potato Curry

Prep time: 10 minutes | Cook time: 30 minutes | Serves 2

2 large potatoes, peeled and diced

1 small onion, peeled and diced

8 ounces (227 g) fresh tomatoes

1 tablespoon olive oil

1 cup water

2 tablespoons grated garlic cloves, divided

½ tablespoon rosemary

½ tablespoon cayenne pepper

1½ tablespoons thyme

Salt and pepper, to taste

1. Pour the water into the pressure cooker and place the trivet inside. 2. Place the potatoes and 1 tablespoon of the garlic over the trivet and sprinkle some salt and pepper on top. 3. Close and lock the pressure cooker lid. Select the Steam mode and set the cooking time for 20 minutes on High Pressure. Press Start. Once the timer goes off, perform a natural pressure release for 15 minutes, then release any remaining pressure. Carefully open the lid. 4. Put the potatoes to one side and empty the cooker. 5. Select the Sauté mode. Add the remaining ingredients to the cooker and cook for 10 minutes. Use an immerse blender to purée the cooked mixture. 6. Stir in the steamed potatoes and serve hot.

Cauliflower Butternut Squash

Prep time: 10 minutes | Cook time: 7 minutes | Serves 3

½ medium onion, diced	butternut squash
2 teaspoons oil	½ cup vegetable broth
1 garlic clove, minced	½ teaspoon paprika
½ cup tomato paste	¼ teaspoon dried thyme
½ pound (227 g) frozen cauliflower	2 tablespoons chopped fresh cilantro
½ pound (227 g) frozen, cubed	2 pinches sea salt

1. Press the Sauté button on the pressure cooker and heat the oil. Add the onion and garlic into the pressure cooker and sauté for 2 minutes. 2. Add the broth, tomato paste, cauliflower, butternut, and all the spices, to the pot. 3. Close and lock the pressure cooker lid. Select the Pressure Cook and set the cooking time for 5 minutes on High Pressure. Press Start. When the timer goes off, do a quick pressure release. Carefully open the lid. 4. Stir well, garnish with the fresh cilantro and serve hot.

Steamed Vegetables

Prep time: 5 minutes | Cook time: 7 minutes | Serves 2 to 4

3 small zucchinis, sliced	1 tablespoon Italian seasoning
1 cup water	Salt, to taste
2 bell peppers, sliced	2 tablespoons olive oil
½ cup minced garlic	

1. Pour the water and insert the trivet into the pressure cooker. 2. In a large bowl, combine the zucchinis, peppers, and garlic. 3. Season the veggies with Italian seasoning, salt and oil. Stir well. 4. Place the vegetables on the trivet. 5. Close and lock the pressure cooker lid. Select the Steam mode and set the cooking time for 7 minutes on High Pressure. Press Start. When the timer goes off, do a quick pressure release. Carefully open the lid. 6. Serve.

Tofu Steaks with Paprika

Prep time: 20 minutes | Cook time: 20 minutes | Serves 4

1 (16-ounces / 454-g) package firm tofu

1 tablespoon olive oil

1 teaspoon dried Italian seasoning

½ teaspoon smoked paprika

¼ teaspoon garlic powder

¼ teaspoon sea salt

⅛ teaspoon red pepper flakes

1. Drain the liquid from the tofu. Place the tofu on some paper towels. Top with more paper towels and press gently but firmly to remove more liquid. Repeat this step, then cut the tofu into four equal-size slices. 2. In a glass baking dish large enough to hold the tofu slices, whisk together the olive oil, Italian seasoning, paprika, garlic powder, salt, and red pepper flakes. Add the tofu to the dish and turn to coat. Let stand for 10 minutes. 3. Put two of the tofu slices in the air fryer basket. Add a raised rack and put the other two tofu slices on the rack. 4. Close and lock the air fryer lid. Select Bake, set temperature to 375°F (191°C), and set time to 15 to 20 minutes. Press Start. It will be done until the tofu is golden brown. Serve.

Tomato Cheese Sandwiches

Prep time: 10 minutes | Cook time: 18 minutes | Serves 4

1⅓ cups shredded vegan Mozzarella cheese

¼ cup chopped oil-packed sun-dried tomatoes, drained

8 slices whole-wheat bread

2 tablespoons egg replacer

⅓ cup coconut milk

1 teaspoon dried Italian seasoning

½ cup dried Italian flavored bread crumbs

1. Divide the Mozzarella cheese and sun-dried tomatoes among four slices of bread. Top each with a slice of bread. Try to keep the cheese away from the edges

of the bread. 2. In a shallow bowl wide enough to hold a sandwich, whisk together the egg replacer, milk, and Italian seasoning until smooth. Place the bread crumbs in another shallow bowl. 3. Carefully dip the sandwiches into the mixture, turning once. Dip each sandwich into the bread crumbs, gently patting the bread crumbs down so they stick to the mixture. 4. Place two sandwiches in a single layer in the air fryer basket. Close and lock the air fryer lid. Select Bake, set temperature to 400°F (204°C), and set time to 5 minutes. Press Start. Carefully turn the sandwiches over and bake for another 4 minutes or until the bread is golden and the cheese is melted. Repeat with remaining sandwiches. Cut into halves and serve.

Spinach Cheese Calzones

Prep time: 7 minutes | Cook time: 10 minutes | Makes 2 Calzones

¼ basic whole wheat bread dough

½ cup vegan Mozzarella or Ricotta

½ cup chopped greens or spinach

Small amounts of any other fillings you want to add, like roasted garlic; roasted peppers; or chopped olives, tomatoes or summer squash

Tomato sauce, for serving

1. Divide the dough into 2 pieces and roll into thin ovals. You don't want the dough so thin that it tears. When I'm rolling the dough out I keep flipping it so it doesn't stick to the cutting board. 2. Spread the cheese on half the dough, then pile on your toppings. Repeat with the second calzone. Fold the dough over to make a half-moon shape, then crimp the dough around the edges to seal well. 3. Place the calzone into air fryer basket. You may need to work in batches. Close and lock the air fryer lid. Select Bake, set temperature to 350°F (177°C), and set time to 5 minutes. Press Start. Turn over and cook 5 minutes more. Repeat with the other calzone. 4. Serve sliced in half with a side of warm tomato sauce.

Cheese Stuffed Potato

Prep time: 15 minutes | Cook time: 35 to 40 minutes | Serves 2

2 medium russet potatoes, scrubbed

1 cup leftover homemade chili or stew or 1 (15-ounces / 425-g) can vegan chili or stew

½ cup nondairy shredded cheddar or Mozzarella cheese

¼ cup nondairy sour cream

2 tablespoons finely chopped chives

1. Pierce the potatoes with a fork and arrange them in the air fryer basket. Close and lock the air fryer lid. Select Bake, set temperature to 390°F (199°C), and set time to 30 minutes. Press Start. 2. Heat the chili on the stovetop or in the microwave until it is hot. 3. Carefully remove the potatoes from the basket and slice them lengthwise without cutting all the way through. Spoon ½ cup of the hot chili into each potato. Add ¼ cup cheese over each potato. 4. Return the potatoes to the basket and continue baking at 390°F (199°C) for 5 to 10 minutes longer. Serve the potatoes with a dollop of sour cream and chives.

Eggplant Cheese Casserole

Prep time: 30 minutes | Cook time: 23 minutes | Serves 2

1 large eggplant, peeled and diced

1 tablespoon olive oil

½ teaspoon dried oregano

1 teaspoon kosher salt

¼ teaspoon freshly ground black pepper

1½ cups marinara sauce

½ cup vegan Ricotta-style cheese

¾ cup shredded vegan Mozzarella-style cheese

3 tablespoons panko bread crumbs

1. Spray a baking pan with nonstick cooking spray. Set aside. 2. In a large bowl, combine the eggplant, olive oil, oregano, salt, and pepper. Toss well to coat. 3. Place the eggplant in the fryer basket. Close and lock the air fryer lid. Select , set

temperature to 400°F (204°C), and set time to 10 minutes. Press Start. It will be done until tender and starting to brown. Remove the eggplant from the fryer basket and be sure to clean out any pieces of eggplant. 4. Place half the eggplant in the pan and top with half the marinara sauce, Ricotta, and Mozzarella. Repeat with the remaining eggplant, sauce, and cheeses. 5. Place the pan in the fryer basket. Close and lock the air fryer lid and baking at 400°F (204°C) for 10 minutes. 6. Remove the pan from the air fryer basket and top the casserole with the bread crumbs. 7. Return the pan to the fryer basket and cook until the bread crumbs are golden brown, about 2 to 3 minutes more. 8. Remove the pan from the fryer basket and allow the casserole to cool for 5 to 10 minutes before serving.

Tater Tot Casserole with Cheese

Prep time: 15 minutes | Cook time: 15 minutes | Serves 4

10 ounces (283g) vegan frozen tater tots

1 tablespoon vegan butter

1 tablespoon all-purpose flour

½ cup unsweetened soy milk

¾ teaspoon kosher salt

2 cups mixed vegetables (fresh or frozen and thawed)

½ cup shredded vegan Cheddar-style cheese

1. Spray a baking dish with nonstick cooking spray. Set aside. 2. Place the tater tots in the fryer basket. Close and lock the air fryer lid. Select Bake, set temperature to 400°F (204°C), and set time to 5 minutes. Press Start. Transfer the tater tots to a bowl and set aside. Clean out any crumbs from the fryer basket. 3. In a small saucepan on the stovetop over medium heat, melt the butter. Add the flour and cook for 2 to 3 minutes. Whisk in the soy milk. Add the salt and vegetables. Mix well. 4. Place the vegetable mixture in the dish and top with the partially cooked tater tots. 5. Place the dish in the fryer basket. Close and lock the air fryer lid and bake at 400°F (204°C) for 5 minutes. Pause the machine and sprinkle the cheese over the top. Restart the machine and bake for 5 minutes more. 6. Remove the dish from the fryer basket and allow the casserole to cool for

10 minutes before serving.

Pineapple Brown Rice Bake

Prep time: 4 minutes | Cook time: 6 to 8 minutes | Serves 2 to 4

1 teaspoon sesame oil

⅓ cup chopped onion

⅓ cup chopped bell pepper

2 cups cooked brown rice

1 (8-ounces / 227-g) can crushed pineapple, drained

½ teaspoon salt

1. Add the oil, onion, and bell pepper in a baking pan, and place the pan into air fryer basket. Close and lock the air fryer lid. Select Bake, set temperature to 390°F (199°C), and set time to 1 minute. Press Start. Open the lid and stir. 2. Lock the lid again and bake the veggie mixture for 3 to 4 more minutes or just until the vegetables become tender. 3. Transfer the vegetables to a bowl and add the rice, pineapple, and salt, stirring until well mixed. 4. Pour the mixture back into the air fryer baking pan and bake at 390°F (199°C) for 2 to 3 minutes, until everything heats through.

Chapter 7 Salads

Sweet Potato Salad with Parsley

Prep time: 10 minutes | Cook time: 17 minutes | Serves 4

¼ cup olive oil

1 medium yellow onion, peeled and diced

2 cloves garlic, minced

1 teaspoon ground cumin

1 teaspoon paprika

¼ cup fresh lemon juice

1 cup water

3 cups peeled and cubed sweet potatoes

¼ cup chopped green olives

3 tablespoons chopped fresh Italian flat-leaf parsley

Pinch of salt   Pinch of freshly ground black pepper

1. Press the Sauté button on the pressure cooker and heat the oil. Add the onion and sauté for 5 minites, or until it begins to turn golden brown. Add the garlic, cumin, paprika, and lemon juice and cook for about 2 minutes. Transfer to a large bowl and set aside. 2. Add the water and the sweet potatoes to the cooker. 3. Close and lock the pressure cooker lid. Select the Pressure Cook and set the cooking time for 10 minutes on High Pressure. Press Start. Once the timer goes off, perform a natural pressure release for 10 minutes, then release any remaining pressure. Carefully open the lid. 4. Drain the sweet potatoes in a colander. Toss the potatoes with the onion mixture. Add the olives and parsley and season with salt and pepper, and serve warm.

Apple and Celery Barley Salad

Prep time: 10 minutes | Cook time: 20 minutes | Serves 2 to 4

2½ cups water

1 cup pearl barley, rinsed

Salt and white pepper, to taste

1 green apple, chopped

¼ cup chopped celery

¾ cup jarred spinach pesto

1. Combine the water, barley, salt, and white pepper into the pressure cooker. 2. Close and lock the pressure cooker lid. Select the Pressure Cook and set the cooking time for 20 minutes at High Pressure. Press Start. 3. When the timer beeps, perform a quick pressure release. Carefully remove the lid. 4. Drain the barley and transfer to a bowl. Add the chopped apple, celery, and spinach pesto,

2. tossing to coat, and serve.

Blueberry Wheat Berry Salad

Prep time: 10 minutes | Cook time: 25 minutes | Serves 4

1½ cup wheat berries, soaked overnight

4 cups water

¼ cup walnut oil

¼ cup apple cider vinegar

1 tablespoon Dijon mustard

½ teaspoon salt

½ teaspoon black pepper

½ cup minced red onion

1 cup fresh blueberries

½ cup sliced almonds

1. Drain the excess water off the soaked wheat berries and place them into the pressure cooker. Add in the water and stir. 2. Close and lock the pressure cooker lid. Select the Pressure Cook and set the cooking time for 25 minutes on High Pressure. Press Start. Once the timer goes off, perform a natural pressure release for 15 minutes, then release any remaining pressure. 3. While the steam is releasing, combine the walnut oil, apple cider vinegar, Dijon mustard, salt and black pepper. Whisk together until thoroughly combined. 4. Carefully open the lid. Remove the cooked wheat berries from the pot. Add the dressing and stir. 5. Cover and place in the refrigerator for at least 1 hour to chill. 6. Remove the wheat berries from the refrigerator and fluff with a fork. 7. Add the blueberries and almonds and stir gently before serving.

Pomegranate Brussels Sprout Salad

Prep time: 5 minutes | Cook time: 5 minutes | Serves 8

2 pounds (907 g) Brussels sprouts, trimmed and halved

1 tablespoon unsalted vegan butter, melted

1 cup water

2 cups pomegranate seeds

½ cup chopped almonds

1. Pour the water and insert the trivet into the pressure cooker. Arrange the Brussels sprouts on the trivet. 2. Close and lock the pressure cooker lid. Select the Pressure Cook and set the cooking time for 5 minutes on High Pressure. Press Start. Once the timer goes off, perform a natural pressure release for 5 minutes, then release any remaining pressure. Carefully open the lid. 3. Transfer the sprouts to a platter and pour the melted butter on top. 4. Sprinkle the almonds and pomegranate seeds on top and serve.

Beet and Carrot Salad

Prep time: 10 minutes | Cook time: 10 minutes | Serves 4

2 medium beets, peeled and diced

1 tablespoon olive oil, divided

½ teaspoon kosher salt, divided

8 cups mixed greens

Crispy garlic chickpeas

1 cup grated carrots

1 cup crumbly vegan havarti-style or Monterey Jack–style cheese

The Dressing:

2 tablespoons olive oil

1 tablespoon balsamic vinegar

½ teaspoon kosher salt

½ teaspoon freshly ground black pepper

1. In a large bowl, make the dressing by whisking together the ingredients. Set aside. 2. In a separate large bowl, combine the beets, olive oil, and salt. Toss well to coat. 3. Place the beets in the fryer basket. Close and lock the air fryer lid. Select Air Fry, set temperature to 400°F (204°C), and set time to 8 to 10 minutes. Press Start. 4. Transfer the beets to a platter and allow to cool for 10 minutes. Place the greens on top of the dressing. Add the beets, chickpeas, carrots, and cheese. Toss well to coat and serve immediately.

Spinach Veggie Burger Salad

Prep time: 10 minutes | Cook time: 11 minutes | Serves 4

4 veggie burgers

2 cups cubed whole grain bread

2 teaspoons olive oil

2 teaspoons everything bagel seasoning

8 cups baby spinach

1 cup sliced strawberries

2 cups diced cucumber

½ cup favorite salad dressing

1. Place the burgers in the fryer basket. Close and lock the air fryer lid. Select

Bake, set temperature to 390°F (199°C), and set time to 8 minutes (4 minutes per side). Press Start. Remove the burgers from the fryer basket and roughly chop. Set aside. 2. Place the bread in a large bowl and drizzle with the olive oil. 3. Place the cubes in the fryer basket. Close and lock the air fryer lid and bake at 390°F (199°C) for 2 to 3 minutes, or until toasted. 4. Transfer the croutons to a clean large bowl and add the seasoning. Toss well to coat. 5. In a separate large bowl, combine the spinach, strawberries, and cucumber. Add the croutons, burgers, and dressing. Toss well to coat. 6. Divide the salad into 4 bowls before serving.

Pecan and Apple Salad

Prep time: 15 minutes | Cook time: 14 minutes | Serves 4

2 Granny Smith apples, cored and cut into chunks	2 tablespoons freshly squeezed lemon juice
2 teaspoons olive oil, divided	1 tablespoon honey
1½ cups red grapes	3 celery stalks, sliced
½ cup mayonnaise	½ cup coarsely chopped pecans

1. Put the chopped apples in the air fryer basket and drizzle with 1 teaspoon olive oil; toss to coat. 2. Place the basket in the air fryer. Close and lock the air fryer lid. Select Roast, set temperature to 400°F (204°C), and set time to 4 minutes. Press Start. Remove the basket. 3. Add the grapes to the basket and drizzle with the remaining 1 teaspoon of olive oil; toss again. Return the basket to the cooker and roast for 8 to 10 minutes longer, shaking the basket halfway through cooking time, until tender. 4. Meanwhile, whisk together the mayonnaise, lemon juice, and honey in a medium bowl. 5. Add the celery and pecans to the dressing and stir to combine. 6. Place the roasted apples and grapes in the bowl and stir gently to coat the fruit with the dressing. Serve or refrigerate for 2 hours before serving.

Squash and Asparagus Salad

Prep time: 15 minutes | Cook time: 11 minutes | Serves 4

1 yellow summer squash, sliced

1½ cups (2-inch pieces) fresh asparagus

1 orange bell pepper, sliced

1 cup sliced button mushrooms

4 tablespoons olive oil, divided

½ teaspoon sea salt

2 tablespoons freshly squeezed lemon juice

1 tablespoon freshly squeezed orange juice

1 tablespoon honey mustard

1 teaspoon dried thyme

1. Put the squash, asparagus, bell pepper, and mushrooms in the air fryer basket and toss to mix. Drizzle the vegetables with 1 tablespoon of olive oil and sprinkle with the salt. Put the basket in the air fryer. 2. Close and lock the air fryer lid. Select Roast, set temperature to 375°F (191°C), and set time to 8 to 11 minutes. Press Start. Toss halfway through cooking time, until the vegetables are tender. 3. Meanwhile, in a large serving bowl whisk together the remaining 3 tablespoons of olive oil, lemon juice, orange juice, mustard, and thyme. 4. When the vegetables are done, add them to the serving bowl and toss to coat with the dressing. Serve immediately, at room temperature, or chill for a few hours before serving.

Corn and Black Bean Salad

Prep time: 18 minutes | Cook time: 12 minutes | Serves 6

1 tablespoon light olive oil

½ teaspoon garlic powder

½ teaspoon cumin

2 small ears corn

1 cup cooked black beans

½ cup slivered poblano peppers

½ medium red or white onion

1 small avocado

3 tablespoons lime juice

¼ teaspoon salt

1. In a small bowl, mix the olive oil, garlic powder, and cumin. 2. Remove the husks and silk from the ears of corn. 3. Brush the oil mixture over all surfaces of the corn. 4. Place the corn in the air fryer basket. Close and lock the air fryer lid. Select Bake, set temperature to 390°F (199°C), and set time to 10 to 12 minutes. Press Start. 5. While the corn is cooking, slice the poblano peppers into small slivers, ⅛-inch wide, and then dice the onion. 6. When the corn has finished cooking, place the ears on a cutting board, stem end down, and cut or scrape the kernels from the cobs. 7. Dice the avocado into ¼-inch cubes. 8. Toss the corn, beans, peppers, onion, and avocado together with the lime juice and salt.

Crabless Cake Salad with Pineapple

Prep time: 10 minutes | Cook time: 10 minutes | Serves 4

2 (8-ounce / 227-g) packages crabless cakes (10 count)

Oil for misting or cooking spray

1 cup minced pineapple

⅓ cup minced red onion

⅓ cup minced bell pepper, any color

4 cups shredded cabbage

1. Mist all sides of the crab cakes with oil or cooking spray and place them in the air fryer basket. 2. Close and lock the air fryer lid. Select Bake, set temperature to 390°F (199°C), and set time to 10 minutes. Press Start. It will be done until they turn brown and crisp. 3. Meanwhile, prepare the pineapple, red onion, and bell pepper and stir them together to make the salsa. 4. On each of 4 salad plates, place 1 cup of shredded cabbage. 5. Divide the salsa evenly over the cabbage. 6. Arrange 5 of the cooked cakes on each plate to serve.

Chapter 8 Desserts

Cinnamon Balls

Prep time: 15 minutes | Cook time: 20 minutes | Serves 8

¼ cup whole-wheat flour

½ cup all-purpose flour

½ teaspoon baking powder

3 tablespoons sugar, divided

¼ teaspoon plus ½ tablespoon cinnamon

¼ teaspoon sea salt

2 tablespoons cold vegan butter, cubed

⅓ cup almond milk

1 cup water

1. Mix the whole-wheat flour, all-purpose flour, baking powder, 1 tablespoon of sugar, ¼ teaspoon of cinnamon, and salt in a medium bowl. 2. Add the butter and use a pastry cutter to cut into butter, breaking it into little pieces until resembling cornmeal. Pour in the milk and mix until the dough forms into a ball. 3. Knead the dough on a flat surface. Divide the dough into 8 pieces and roll each piece into a ball. Put the balls in a greased baking pan with space in between each ball and oil the balls. 4. Pour the water into the pressure cooker. Put in a trivet and place the pan on top. 5. SClose and lock the pressure cooker lid. Select the Pressure Cook and set the time for 20 minutes on High Pressure. Press Start. 6. When timer beeps, perform a natural pressure release for 5 minutes, then release any remaining pressure. 7. In a mixing bowl, combine the remaining sugar and cinnamon. Toss the dough balls in the cinnamon and sugar mixture to serve.

Apple Pie

Prep time: 20 minutes | Cook time: 30 minutes | Serves 8

2 apples, chopped

Juice of 1 lemon

3 tablespoons sugar

1 teaspoon vanilla extract

1 teaspoon cornstarch

1 (2-crust) box refrigerated pie crusts

1 cup water

1. In a mixing bowl, combine the apples, lemon juice, sugar, and vanilla. Allow the mixture to stand for 10 minutes, then drain and reserve 1 tablespoon of the liquid. 2. In another bowl, whisk the cornstarch into the reserved liquid and mix with the apple mixture. 3. Put the pie crusts on a lightly floured surface and cut into 8 circles. Spoon a tablespoon of apple mixture in the center of the circle. Brush the edges with some water and fold the dough over the filling. 4. Press the edges with a fork to seal. Cut 3 small slits on top of each pie and grease with cooking spray. 5. Arrange the cakes in a single layer in a greased baking pan. Pour the water into the pressure cooker. Fit in a trivet and place the pan on top. 6. Close and lock the pressure cooker lid. Select the Pressure Cook and set the cooking time for 30 minutes on High Pressure. Press Start. 7. When timer beeps, perform a natural pressure release for 10 minutes, then release the remaining pressure, and unlock the lid. 8. Serve immediately.

Fudgy Chocolate Brownies

Prep time: 10 minutes | Cook time: 5 minutes | Makes 3 brownies

2 cups water

3 ounces (85 g) dairy-free dark chocolate

1 tablespoon coconut oil

½ cup applesauce

2 tablespoons unrefined sugar

⅓ cup all-purpose flour

½ teaspoon baking powder

Salt, to taste

1. Pour the water into the pressure cooker and insert a trivet. Select Sauté. 2. Stir together the chocolate and coconut oil in a large bowl. Place the bowl on the trivet. Stir occasionally until the chocolate is melted, then turn off the pressure cooker. 3. Stir the applesauce and sugar into the chocolate mixture. Add the flour, baking powder, and salt and stir just until combined. Pour the batter into 3 ramekins. Cover each ramekin with aluminum foil. Using a foil sling or silicone helper handles, lower the ramekins onto the trivet. 4. Close and lock the pressure cooker lid. Select the Pressure Cook and set the cooking time for 5 minutes at High Pressure. Press Start. 5. When the timer beeps, perform a quick pressure release. Carefully remove the lid. 6. Cool for 5 to 10 minutes before serving.

Lemon Blueberry Cheesecake

Prep time: 10 minutes | Cook time: 6 minutes | Serves 6

1 tablespoon coconut oil, melted, for greasing the pan

1¼ cups soft pitted Medjool dates, divided

1 cup gluten-free rolled oats

2 cups cashews

1 cup fresh blueberries

3 tablespoons freshly squeezed lemon juice or lime juice

1¾ cups water

Salt, to taste

1. Grease a 6-inch springform pan or pie dish with melted coconut oil. 2. In a food processor, combine 1 cup of dates and the oats. Processor until they form a sticky mixture. Press this mixture into the prepared pan. 3. In a blender, combine the remaining ¼ cup of dates, cashews, blueberries, lemon juice, ¾ cup of water, and a pinch of salt. Blend on high speed for about 1 minute, until smooth and creamy, stopping a couple of times to scrape down the sides. Pour this mixture over the crust. Cover the pan with aluminum foil. 4. Pour the remaining 1 cup of water into the pressure cooker and insert a trivet. Using a foil sling or silicone helper handles, lower the pan onto the trivet. 5. Close and lock the pressure cooker lid. Select the Pressure Cook and set the cooking time for 6 minutes at High Pressure. Press Start. 6. When the timer beeps, perform a natural pressure release for 10 minutes, then release any remaining pressure. Carefully remove the lid. 7. Cool for 5 to 10 minutes before slicing and serving.

Pear and Apple Smoothie

Prep time: 2 minutes | Cook time: 4 minutes | Makes 3 cups

2 (1-pound / 454-g) large firm but ripe pears, peeled, quartered, and cored

2 (1-pound / 454-g) large apples, peeled, quartered, and cored

¼ cup apple juice

1. Combine all the ingredients into the pressure cooker. Close and lock the pressure cooker lid. Select the Steam setting and set the cooking time for 4

minutes at low pressure. Press Start. 2. When timer beeps, let the pressure release naturally for 3 minutes, then release any remaining pressure. Open the lid. 3. Use a hand mixer to break the pears and apples to make the smoothie. 4. Serve immediately.

Rhubarb and Strawberry Compote

Prep time: 10 minutes | Cook time: 5 minutes | Makes 4 cups

1 pound (454 g) rhubarb (about 4 large stalks), trimmed and cut into 1-inch pieces

1 pound (454 g) strawberries, hulled and quartered lengthwise

½ cup turbinado sugar

½ teaspoon ground cardamom

1. Combine the rhubarb, strawberries, sugar, and cardamom into the pressure cooker and stir well, making sure to coat the rhubarb and strawberries evenly with the sugar. Let the mixture sit for 15 minutes. Stir. 2. Close and lock the pressure cooker lid. Select the Pressure Cook and set the cooking time for 5 minutes at Low Pressure. Press Start. 3. When timer beeps, let the pressure release naturally for about 15 minutes, then release any remaining pressure. Open the lid and stir the compote to break down the rhubarb. 4. Serve the compote warm.

Simple Peppermint Hot Chocolate

Prep time: 2 minutes | Cook time: 9 minutes | Serves 4

4 cups coconut milk

¼ cup cocoa powder

¾ teaspoon peppermint extract

6 tablespoons turbinado sugar

¼ teaspoon fine sea salt

1. Combine the milk, cocoa powder, peppermint extract, sugar, and salt into the pressure cooker and whisk to mix well. 2. Select the Sauté setting and set the cooking time for 9 minutes. Close the pressure cooker lid. Press Start. 3. After 4 minutes, open the lid, whisk the mixture for 1 minute, then cover and keep cooking. 4. When the timer goes off, give the hot chocolate a final whisk. 5. Ladle the hot chocolate into mugs and serve.

Vanilla Rice Pudding with Cherries

Prep time: 5 minutes | Cook time: 30 minutes | Serves 6

1 cup short-grain brown rice

1¾ cups coconut milk, plus more as needed

1½ cups water

4 tablespoons unrefined sugar or pure maple syrup, plus more as needed

1 teaspoon vanilla extract

Salt, to taste

¼ cup dried cherries or ½ cup fresh or frozen pitted cherries

1. Combine the rice, milk, water, sugar, vanilla, and salt into the pressure cooker. 2. Close and lock the pressure cooker lid. Select the Pressure Cook and set the cooking time for 30 minutes at High Pressure. Press Start. 3. When the timer beeps, perform a natural pressure release for 20 minutes, then release any remaining pressure. Carefully remove the lid. 4. Stir in the cherries and rest the lid back on (no need to lock it), and let sit for about 10 minutes. 5. Serve with more milk or sugar, as needed.

Chocolate Butter Cookie

Prep time: 15 minutes | Cook time: 18 minutes | Serves 4

½ cup brown sugar

⅓ cup vegan butter, at room temperature

1 tablespoon egg replacer

1 teaspoon vanilla

1 cup all-purpose flour

½ teaspoon baking powder

¼ teaspoon sea salt

Nonstick baking spray containing flour

5 fun size chocolate, nut, and caramel candy bars

1. In a medium bowl, combine the brown sugar, butter, egg replacer, and vanilla and mix well. 2. Add the flour, baking powder, and salt and mix just until a dough forms. 3. Spray a 7-inch round pan with the baking spray, line with parchment

paper on the bottom, and spray the paper. 4. Divide the dough in half. Put half of the dough into the pan and spread out to the edges, patting gently. 5. Slice the candy bars into ½-inch pieces and put them on the dough in the pan, keeping them away from the edges. 6. Top the candy bar slices with the remaining dough and smooth out, being sure to cover all of the candy. Press down on the edges lightly to make sure the dough is sealed. 7. Put the pan in the air fryer basket. Close and lock the air fryer lid. Select Air Fry, set temperature to 350ºF (177ºC), and set time to 13 to 18 minutes. Press Start. Check after 13 minutes, until the cookie is golden brown and set. 8. Take the basket out of the air fryer, then carefully remove the pan and cool on a wire rack for 10 to 15 minutes before you attempt to remove the cookie. Serve whole. Let people break off pieces to eat.

Cherry Tomatoes

Prep time: 13 minutes | Cook time: 3 hours | Makes 1 pint

1 pint (280 to 310 g) cherry or grape tomatoes, halved lengthwise

1. Place the tomato halves cut-side up in your air fryer basket. Close and lock the air fryer lid. Select Dehydrate, set temperature to 150ºF (66ºC), and set time to 1 hour. Press Start. Check, then cook again for 1 hour. 2. The tomato halves should be dry enough to shake now but will still need to dry out more to store them, so shake and cook 1 hour more. 3. Shake again and check for doneness. If you are using in a cooked dish, they can be a little soft, but if you're using them in the tomato powder, they need to be bone dry, so you will cook an additional 30 minutes to 1 hour more. 4. Store in an airtight container.

Vanilla Yogurt Cake

Prep time: 10 minutes | Cook time: 25 to 30 minutes | Serves 8

Oil for misting or cooking spray

1 tablespoon egg replacer

2 tablespoons water

½ cup sugar

¼ cup plus 3 tablespoons self-rising flour

3 tablespoons cocoa

¼ teaspoon baking soda

¼ teaspoon salt

2 tablespoons vegan oil

1 (5.3-ounce / 150 g) container vegan vanilla yogurt

¼ cup nut milk of choice

1. Spray the baking pan with oil or cooking spray and set aside. 2. In a medium bowl, using a wire whisk, whisk together the egg replacer and water. 3. Add the remaining ingredients and whisk until smooth. 4. Pour the batter into the baking pan and place into air fryer basket. Close and lock the air fryer lid. Select Bake, set temperature to 330°F (166°C), and set time to 25 to 30 minutes. Press Start. and cook for 25 to 30 minutes, until a toothpick inserted into the center comes out clean. 5. Let the cake rest for 10 minutes before removing it from the pan.

Peach Yogurt Pudding Cake

Prep time: 10 minutes | Cook time: 35 minutes | Serves 8

1 (8-ounce / 227-g) can diced peaches packed in juice, drained

Oil for misting or cooking spray

1 tablespoon egg replacer

2 tablespoons water

1 cup self-rising flour

¼ teaspoon baking soda

½ cup sugar

2 tablespoons oil

1 (5.3-ounce / 150 g) container vegan peach yogurt

¼ cup almond milk

¼ teaspoon almond extract

1. On several layers of paper towels, place the drained peaches in a single layer and top with more paper towels to remove the excess moisture. 2. Spray the air fryer baking pan with oil or cooking spray. 3. In a medium bowl, using a wire

whisk, mix the egg replacer with the water. 4. Add the remaining ingredients, including the peaches, and whisk until well mixed. 5. Pour the batter into the baking pan and place into the air fryer basket. Close and lock the air fryer lid. Select Bake, set temperature to 330°F (166°C), and set time to 35 minutes. Press Start. It will be done until a toothpick inserted into the center of the cake comes out clean. 6. Let the cake rest for 10 minutes before removing it from the baking pan.

Chocolate and Banana Rolls

Prep time: 10 minutes | Cook time: 6 minutes | Serves 4

4 rice roll wrappers

4 tablespoons vegan chocolate and hazelnut spread or nut butter

2 small bananas, halved

Powdered sugar, to taste

1. Place 1 wrapper on a flat surface, with the pointed end facing up. Spread the butter in the middle and top with half a banana. Fold in the sides over the filling and then roll up from bottom to top. Repeat this step with the remaining wrappers and filling. Spray the rolls with canola oil. 2. Place the rolls in the fryer basket. Close and lock the air fryer lid. Select Bake, set temperature to 370°F (188°C), and set time to 5 to 6 minutes. Press Start. Turn once halfway through. 3. Transfer the rolls to a platter and allow to cool for at least 10 minutes. Dust with the powdered sugar before serving.

Peach Butter Cobbler

Prep time: 6 minutes | Cook time: 8 minutes | Serves 1

½ cup chopped frozen peaches or blueberries

½ cup granola or muesli

½ teaspoon cold vegan butter, cut into small cubes

1. Layer the peaches, granola, and butter in a small air fryer–safe casserole dish. Cover the dish with a heatproof lid or foil. Place into the air fryer basket. 2. Close and lock the air fryer lid. Select Air Fry, set temperature to 390°F (199°C), and set time to 6 minutes. Press Start. Remove the cover and cook at 390°F (199°C) for 2 minutes longer.

Cake with Cocoa

Prep time: 6 minutes | Cook time: 10 minutes | Serves 1

3 tablespoons unbleached all-purpose flour

1½ tablespoons cocoa powder

1 tablespoon plus 1 teaspoon sugar

¼ teaspoon baking powder

⅛ teaspoon salt

3 teaspoons applesauce

3 tablespoons almond milk

½ teaspoon vanilla extract

1 to 2 spritzes canola oil

Simple coco whip, for serving (optional)

1. In a medium bowl, combine the flour, cocoa powder, sugar, baking powder, and salt. 2. In a small bowl, combine the applesauce, milk, and vanilla. Pour the applesauce mixture over the flour mixture and stir until there are no lumps in the batter. 3. Spritz a small ramekin or baking pan with the oil (if you are omitting the oil, use a nonstick pan). Pour the batter into the ramekin. 4. Place the ramekin into air fryer basket. Close and lock the air fryer lid. Select , set temperature to 360°F (182°C), and set time to 7 to 10 minutes. Press Start. The cake is done when you insert a toothpick into the center and it comes out clean. When the cake is cool, serve with the coco whip, if desired.

Chapter 9 Staples, Sauces and Dips

White Sauce

Prep time: 5 minutes | Cook time: 8 to 9 minutes | Makes 3 cups

½ cup vegan butter	1 teaspoon salt
½ cup all-purpose flour	1 teaspoon freshly ground black pepper
4 cups unsweetened soy milk, warmed	

1. Press the Sauté button on the pressure cooker and melt the butter. Add the flour and stir for 1 to 2 minutes to create a roux. 2. Gradually add the warmed milk to the pot, whisking until there are no lumps. 3. Close and lock the pressure cooker lid. Select the Pressure Cook and set the cooking time for 7 minutes on High Pressure. Press Start. Once the timer goes off, perform a natural pressure release for 10 minutes, then release any remaining pressure. Carefully open the lid. 5. Season with salt and pepper. Serve immediately. Store any remaining mixture in an airtight container with a tight-fitting lid in the refrigerator up to 2 days.

Red Pepper Sauce

Prep time: 5 minutes | Cook time: 7 minutes | Serves 4

2 cups roasted red peppers	1 teaspoon garlic powder
2 cups vegetable broth	½ cup fresh basil
2 tablespoons red wine vinegar	Pinch of salt
2 tablespoons extra-virgin olive oil	Pinch of freshly ground black pepper

1. Add the red peppers, broth, vinegar, and oil to a food processor and purée until smooth. Pour the mixture into the pressure cooker. 2. Add the garlic powder to the cooker and stir. 3. Close and lock the pressure cooker lid. Select the Pressure Cook and set the cooking time for 7 minutes on High Pressure. Press Start. Once the timer goes off, perform a natural pressure release for 10 minutes, then release any remaining pressure. Carefully open the lid. 4. Add the basil, salt and pepper before serving. Store remaining mixture in an airtight container with a tight-fitting lid up to 2 to 3 days in the refrigerator or 1 week in the freezer.

Fresh Garden Tomato Salsa

Prep time: 5 minutes | Cook time: 5 minutes | Makes 6 to 8 cups

8 large tomatoes, roughly chopped

6 garlic cloves, finely diced

2 jalapeño peppers, deseeded and diced

1 red bell pepper, diced

1 small red onion, diced

1 small yellow onion, diced

1 tablespoon ground cumin

3 to 4 teaspoons salt

½ teaspoon freshly ground black pepper

½ teaspoon baking soda

¼ cup tomato paste

2 tablespoons freshly squeezed lime juice

1 teaspoon chopped fresh cilantro leaves

1. In the pressure cooker, stir together the tomatoes, garlic, jalapeños, bell pepper, red onion, yellow onion, cumin, salt, pepper, and baking soda. 2. Close and lock the pressure cooker lid. Select the Pressure Cook and set the cooking time for 5 minutes on High Pressure. Press Start. Once the timer goes off, perform a natural pressure release for 10 minutes, then release any remaining pressure. Carefully open the lid. 3. Stir in the tomato paste, lime juice and cilantro. 4. Serve chilled or at room temperature.

Artichoke-Spinach Dip

Prep time: 5 minutes | Cook time: 4 minutes | Makes 2½ cups

1 cup raw cashews

1 cup unsweetened coconut milk

1 tablespoon nutritional yeast

1½ tablespoons apple cider vinegar

1 teaspoon onion powder

½ teaspoon garlic powder

½ to 1 teaspoon salt

1 (14-ounce / 397-g) can artichoke hearts in water

2 cups fresh spinach

1 cup water

1. In a blender, combine the cashews, milk, nutritional yeast, vinegar, onion powder, garlic powder, and salt. Purée until smooth and creamy, about 1 minute. Add the artichoke hearts and spinach and pulse a few times to chop up a bit. Pour the mixture into a baking pan. 2. Pour the water and insert the trivet into the pressure cooker. Put the pan on the trivet. 3. Close and lock the pressure cooker

lid. Select the Pressure Cook and set the cooking time for 4 minutes on High Pressure. Press Start. Once the timer goes off, perform a natural pressure release for 10 minutes, then release any remaining pressure. Carefully open the lid. 4. Let the baking pan cool for a few minutes before carefully lifting it out of the cooker with oven mitts. 5. Transfer the dip to a bowl and serve.

Instant Pot Soy Yogurt

Prep time: 5 minutes | Cook time: 8 hours | Makes 4 cups

1 (32-ounce / 907-g) container plain unsweetened soy milk

1 packet vegan yogurt starter

1 tablespoon tapioca starch

1. Whisk together the soy milk, starter and starch in a mixing bowl. Pour the mixture into small glass jars. Sit them right on the cooker bottom. 2. Close and lock the pressure cooker lid. Select the Slow Cook and set the cooking time for 8 hours. Press Start. When the timer goes off, do a quick pressure release. Carefully open the lid. 3. Serve chilled. Store in the fridge for up to 10 days.

Onion Cream

Prep time: 16 minutes | Cook time: 45 minutes | Makes 1 cup

1 large (150 g) onion (but not so large that it can't fit in your air fryer whole) or 3 small onions

½ teaspoon salt, or to taste

1. Set the whole, unpeeled onion in a baking dish with an onion-size piece of parchment paper in it for easy cleanup. (Do not put directly in your air fryer basket, because it will be a mess to clean up!) Place into the air fryer basket. 2. Close and lock the air fryer lid. Select Air Fry, set temperature to 400°F (204°C), and set time to 25 minutes. Press Start. Check and cook 20 minutes more. Carefully remove the pan and let the onion cool. 3. Once cool, peel the skin off, remove any dark or burned parts of the flesh and remove the ends. 4. Cut in half

and put the pieces into your blender with salt. 5. Store in the refrigerator for up to 4 days.

Coco Whip with Vanilla

Prep time: 5 minutes | Cook time: 0 minutes | Makes 2 cups

1 (13-ounces / 369 g) can full-fat coconut milk

1 tablespoon sugar

1 teaspoon vanilla extract

1. Refrigerate the can of coconut milk overnight. 2. Open the can and scoop out the solid cream into a stand mixer bowl or mixing bowl if you are using an electric mixer. (Reserve any liquid in the can for another use—it's a great addition to breakfast oats or soups.) 3. On high-speed, beat the coconut cream until stiff peaks are formed. Add the sugar and vanilla and beat for 1 minute longer. Serve immediately.

Cauliflower Chorizo

Prep time: 5 minutes | Cook time: 5 minutes | Makes 2 cups

4 cups cauliflower florets

1 tablespoon chorizo spice blend

Salt, to taste (optional)

1. Place the cauliflower florets into air fryer basket. Close and lock the air fryer lid. Select Roast, set temperature to 350°F (177°C), and set time to 5 minutes. Press Start. 2. Pour into your food processor with the Chorizo Spice Blend and salt, if using. Pulse until the cauliflower looks like rice or couscous, small bits. 3. Store in the fridge for up to 3 days, or freeze for up to 2 months.

Chickpea Rolls with Thyme

Prep time: 15 minutes | Cook time: 1 hour | Makes 2 rolls

1 (15-ounces / 425-g) can chickpeas, drained (save liquid for aquafaba)

1½ cups (375 ml) water

¼ cup plus 2 tablespoons nutritional yeast

1 teaspoon salt

1 tablespoon tomato paste

½ teaspoon minced garlic

½ teaspoon dried marjoram

½ teaspoon dried thyme

⅛ teaspoon rosemary powder (or ¼ teaspoon dried rosemary)

1½ cups vital wheat gluten flour

1. Add the chickpeas, water, nutritional yeast, salt, tomato paste, garlic, marjoram, thyme and rosemary into your blender and blend until smooth. 2. Add the vital wheat gluten flour to a mixing bowl and mix in the chickpea liquid mixture. Knead until smooth and elastic. 3. Divide the dough into 2 pieces. Place on a piece of parchment paper and roll each dough piece into a log form, and then roll that up in aluminum foil and twist the ends closed. Place both wrapped logs into your air fryer basket. 4. Close and lock the air fryer lid. Select Bake, set temperature to 330°F (166°C), and set time to 40 minutes. Press Start. Cook for 20 minutes more, check one for doneness (cut in half) and wrap back up and cook more if needed. The crust will be a bit tougher than steamed seitan. 5. Store in the fridge or freeze for later. If you choose to freeze it, cut it first to make it easier to use when you're ready for it.

Appendix 1 Measurement Conversion Chart

MEASUREMENT CONVERSION CHART

VOLUME EQUIVALENTS (DRY)

US STANDARD	METRIC (APPROXIMATE)
1/8 teaspoon	0.5 mL
1/4 teaspoon	1 mL
1/2 teaspoon	2 mL
3/4 teaspoon	4 mL
1 teaspoon	5 mL
1 tablespoon	15 mL
1/4 cup	59 mL
1/2 cup	118 mL
3/4 cup	177 mL
1 cup	235 mL
2 cups	475 mL
3 cups	700 mL
4 cups	1 L

VOLUME EQUIVALENTS (LIQUID)

US STANDARD	US STANDARD (OUNCES)	METRIC (APPROXIMATE)
2 tablespoons	1 fl.oz.	30 mL
1/4 cup	2 fl.oz.	60 mL
1/2 cup	4 fl.oz.	120 mL
1 cup	8 fl.oz.	240 mL
1 1/2 cup	12 fl.oz.	355 mL
2 cups or 1 pint	16 fl.oz.	475 mL
4 cups or 1 quart	32 fl.oz.	1 L
1 gallon	128 fl.oz.	4 L

TEMPERATURES EQUIVALENTS

FAHRENHEIT(F)	CELSIUS(C) (APPROXIMATE)
225 °F	107 °C
250 °F	120 °C
275 °F	135 °C
300 °F	150 °C
325 °F	160 °C
350 °F	180 °C
375 °F	190 °C
400 °F	205 °C
425 °F	220 °C
450 °F	235 °C
475 °F	245 °C
500 °F	260 °C

WEIGHT EQUIVALENTS

US STANDARD	METRIC (APPROXIMATE)
1 ounce	28 g
2 ounces	57 g
5 ounces	142 g
10 ounces	284 g
15 ounces	425 g
16 ounces (1 pound)	455 g
1.5 pounds	680 g
2 pounds	907 g

Appendix 2 Instant Pot Cooking Timetable

Instant Pot Cooking Timetable

Dried Beans, Legumes and Lentils

Dried Beans and Legume	Dry (Minutes)	Soaked (Minutes)
Soy beans	25 – 30	20 – 25
Scarlet runner	20 – 25	10 – 15
Pinto beans	25 – 30	20 – 25
Peas	15 – 20	10 – 15
Navy beans	25 – 30	20 – 25
Lima beans	20 – 25	10 – 15
Lentils, split, yellow (moong dal)	15 – 18	N/A
Lentils, split, red	15 – 18	N/A
Lentils, mini, green (brown)	15 – 20	N/A
Lentils, French green	15 – 20	N/A
Kidney white beans	35 – 40	20 – 25
Kidney red beans	25 – 30	20 – 25
Great Northern beans	25 – 30	20 – 25
Pigeon peas	20 – 25	15 – 20
Chickpeas (garbanzo bean chickpeas)	35 – 40	20 – 25
Cannellini beans	35 – 40	20 – 25
Black-eyed peas	20 – 25	10 – 15
Black beans	20 – 25	10 – 15

Fish and Seafood

Fish and Seafood	Fresh (minutes)	Frozen (minutes)
Shrimp or Prawn	1 to 2	2 to 3
Seafood soup or stock	6 to 7	7 to 9
Mussels	2 to 3	4 to 6
Lobster	3 to 4	4 to 6
Fish, whole (snapper, trout, etc.)	5 to 6	7 to 10
Fish steak	3 to 4	4 to 6
Fish fillet,	2 to 3	3 to 4
Crab	3 to 4	5 to 6

Fruits

Fruits	Fresh (in Minutes)	Dried (in Minutes)
Raisins	N/A	4 to 5
Prunes	2 to 3	4 to 5
Pears, whole	3 to 4	4 to 6
Pears, slices or halves	2 to 3	4 to 5
Peaches	2 to 3	4 to 5
Apricots, whole or halves	2 to 3	3 to 4
Apples, whole	3 to 4	4 to 6
Apples, in slices or pieces	2 to 3	3 to 4

Meat

Meat and Cuts	Cooking Time (minutes)	Meat and Cuts	Cooking Time (minutes)
Veal, roast	35 to 45	Duck, with bones, cut up	10 to 12
Veal, chops	5 to 8	Cornish Hen, whole	10 to 15
Turkey, drumsticks (leg)	15 to 20	Chicken, whole	20 to 25
Turkey, breast, whole, with bones	25 to 30	Chicken, legs, drumsticks, or thighs	10 to 15
Turkey, breast, boneless	15 to 20	Chicken, with bones, cut up	10 to 15
Quail, whole	8 to 10	Chicken, breasts	8 to 10
Pork, ribs	20 to 25	Beef, stew	15 to 20
Pork, loin roast	55 to 60	Beef, shanks	25 to 30
Pork, butt roast	45 to 50	Beef, ribs	25 to 30
Pheasant	20 to 25	Beef, steak, pot roast, round, rump, brisket or blade, small chunks, chuck,	25 to 30
Lamb, stew meat	10 to 15		
Lamb, leg	35 to 45	Beef, pot roast, steak, rump, round, chuck, blade or brisket, large	35 to 40
Lamb, cubes,	10 t0 15		
Ham slice	9 to 12	Beef, ox-tail	40 to 50
Ham picnic shoulder	25 to 30	Beef, meatball	10 to 15
Duck, whole	25 to 30	Beef, dressed	20 to 25

Appendix 3 Instant Pot Cooking Timetable

Vegetables (fresh/frozen)

Vegetable	Fresh (minutes)	Frozen (minutes)	Vegetable	Fresh (minutes)	Frozen (minutes)
Zucchini, slices or chunks	2 to 3	3 to 4	Mixed vegetables	2 to 3	3 to 4
Yam, whole, small	10 to 12	12 to 14	Leeks	2 to 4	3 to 5
Yam, whole, large	12 to 15	15 to 19	Greens (collards, beet greens, spinach, kale, turnip greens, swiss chard) chopped	3 to 6	4 to 7
Yam, in cubes	7 to 9	9 to 11			
Turnip, chunks	2 to 4	4 to 6	Green beans, whole	2 to 3	3 to 4
Tomatoes, whole	3 to 5	5 to 7	Escarole, chopped	1 to 2	2 to 3
Tomatoes, in quarters	2 to 3	4 to 5	Endive	1 to 2	2 to 3
Sweet potato, whole, small	10 to 12	12 to 14	Eggplant, chunks or slices	2 to 3	3 to 4
Sweet potato, whole, large	12 to 15	15 to 19	Corn, on the cob	3 to 4	4 to 5
Sweet potato, in cubes	7 to 9	9 to 11	Corn, kernels	1 to 2	2 to 3
Sweet pepper, slices or chunks	1 to 3	2 to 4	Collard	4 to 5	5 to 6
Squash, butternut, slices or chunks	8 to 10	10 to 12	Celery, chunks	2 to 3	3 to 4
Squash, acorn, slices or chunks	6 to 7	8 to 9	Cauliflower flowerets	2 to 3	3 to 4
Spinach	1 to 2	3 to 4	Carrots, whole or chunked	2 to 3	3 to 4
Rutabaga, slices	3 to 5	4 to 6	Carrots, sliced or shredded	1 to 2	2 to 3
Rutabaga, chunks	4 to 6	6 to 8	Cabbage, red, purple or green, wedges	3 to 4	4 to 5
Pumpkin, small slices or chunks	4 to 5	6 to 7	Cabbage, red, purple or green, shredded	2 to 3	3 to 4
Pumpkin, large slices or chunks	8 to 10	10 to 14	Brussel sprouts, whole	3 to 4	4 to 5
Potatoes, whole, large	12 to 15	15 to 19	Broccoli, stalks	3 to 4	4 to 5
Potatoes, whole, baby	10 to 12	12 to 14	Broccoli, flowerets	2 to 3	3 to 4
Potatoes, in cubes	7 to 9	9 to 11	Beets, small roots, whole	11 to 13	13 to 15
Peas, in the pod	1 to 2	2 to 3	Beets, large roots, whole	20 to 25	25 to 30
Peas, green	1 to 2	2 to 3	Beans, green/yellow or wax, whole, trim ends and strings	1 to 2	2 to 3
Parsnips, sliced	1 to 2	2 to 3			
Parsnips, chunks	2 to 4	4 to 6	Asparagus, whole or cut	1 to 2	2 to 3
Onions, sliced	2 to 3	3 to 4	Artichoke, whole, trimmed without leaves	9 to 11	11 to 13
Okra	2 to 3	3 to 4	Artichoke, hearts	4 to 5	5 to 6

Rice and Grains

Rice & Grain	Water Quantity (Grain: Water ratios)	Cooking Time (in Minutes)	Rice & Grain	Water Quantity (Grain: Water ratios)	Cooking Time (in Minutes)
Wheat berries	1:3	25 to 30	Oats, steel-cut	1:1	10
Spelt berries	1:3	15 to 20	Oats, quick cooking	1:1	6
Sorghum	1:3	20 to 25	Millet	1:1	10 to 12
Rice, wild	1:3	25 to 30	Kamut, whole	1:3	10 to 12
Rice, white	1:1.5	8	Couscous	1:2	5 to 8
Rice, Jasmine	1:1	4 to 10	Corn, dried, half	1:3	25 to 30
Rice, Brown	1:1.3	22 to 28	Congee, thin	1:6 ~ 1:7	15 to 20
Rice, Basmati	1:1.5	4 to 8	Congee, thick	1:4 ~ 1:5	15 to 20
Quinoa, quick cooking	1:2	8	Barley, pot	1:3 ~ 1:4	25 to 30
Porridge, thin	1:6 ~ 1:7	15 to 20	Barley, pearl	1:4	25 to 30

Appendix 4 Air Fryer Cooking Chart

Air Fryer Cooking Chart

Beef

Item	Temp (°F)	Time (mins)	Item	Temp (°F)	Time (mins)
Beef Eye Round Roast (4 lbs.)	400 °F	45 to 55	Meatballs (1-inch)	370 °F	7
Burger Patty (4 oz.)	370 °F	16 to 20	Meatballs (3-inch)	380 °F	10
Filet Mignon (8 oz.)	400 °F	18	Ribeye, bone-in (1-inch, 8 oz)	400 °F	10 to 15
Flank Steak (1.5 lbs.)	400 °F	12	Sirloin steaks (1-inch, 12 oz)	400 °F	9 to 14
Flank Steak (2 lbs.)	400 °F	20 to 28			

Chicken

Item	Temp (°F)	Time (mins)	Item	Temp (°F)	Time (mins)
Breasts, bone in (1 ¼ lb.)	370 °F	25	Legs, bone-in (1 ¾ lb.)	380 °F	30
Breasts, boneless (4 oz)	380 °F	12	Thighs, boneless (1 ½ lb.)	380 °F	18 to 20
Drumsticks (2 ½ lb.)	370 °F	20	Wings (2 lb.)	400 °F	12
Game Hen (halved 2 lb.)	390 °F	20	Whole Chicken	360 °F	75
Thighs, bone-in (2 lb.)	380 °F	22	Tenders	360 °F	8 to 10

Pork & Lamb

Item	Temp (°F)	Time (mins)	Item	Temp (°F)	Time (mins)
Bacon (regular)	400 °F	5 to 7	Pork Tenderloin	370 °F	15
Bacon (thick cut)	400 °F	6 to 10	Sausages	380 °F	15
Pork Loin (2 lb.)	360 °F	55	Lamb Loin Chops (1-inch thick)	400 °F	8 to 12
Pork Chops, bone in (1-inch, 6.5 oz)	400 °F	12	Rack of Lamb (1.5 – 2 lb.)	380 °F	22

Fish & Seafood

Item	Temp (°F)	Time (mins)	Item	Temp (°F)	Time (mins)
Calamari (8 oz)	400 °F	4	Tuna Steak	400 °F	7 to 10
Fish Fillet (1-inch, 8 oz)	400 °F	10	Scallops	400 °F	5 to 7
Salmon, fillet (6 oz)	380 °F	12	Shrimp	400 °F	5
Swordfish steak	400 °F	10			

Appendix 5 Air Fryer Cooking Chart

Air Fryer Cooking Chart

Vegetables

INGREDIENT	AMOUNT	PREPARATION	OIL	TEMP	COOK TIME
Asparagus	2 bunches	Cut in half, trim stems	2 Tbsp	420°F	12-15 mins
Beets	1½ lbs	Peel, cut in ½-inch cubes	1 Tbsp	390°F	28-30 mins
Bell peppers (for roasting)	4 peppers	Cut in quarters, remove seeds	1 Tbsp	400°F	15-20 mins
Broccoli	1 large head	Cut in 1-2-inch florets	1 Tbsp	400°F	15-20 mins
Brussels sprouts	1 lb	Cut in half, remove stems	1 Tbsp	425°F	15-20 mins
Carrots	1 lb	Peel, cut in ¼-inch rounds	1 Tbsp	425°F	10-15 mins
Cauliflower	1 head	Cut in 1-2-inch florets	2 Tbsp	400°F	20-22 mins
Corn on the cob	7 ears	Whole ears, remove husks	1 Tbps	400°F	14-17 mins
Green beans	1 bag (12 oz)	Trim	1 Tbps	420°F	18-20 mins
Kale (for chips)	4 oz	Tear into pieces, remove stems	None	325°F	5-8 mins
Mushrooms	16 oz	Rinse, slice thinly	1 Tbps	390°F	25-30 mins
Potatoes, russet	1½ lbs	Cut in 1-inch wedges	1 Tbps	390°F	25-30 mins
Potatoes, russet	1 lb	Hand-cut fries, soak 30 mins in cold water, then pat dry	½ -3 Tbps	400°F	25-28 mins
Potatoes, sweet	1 lb	Hand-cut fries, soak 30 mins in cold water, then pat dry	1 Tbps	400°F	25-28 mins
Zucchini	1 lb	Cut in eighths lengthwise, then cut in half	1 Tbps	400°F	15-20 mins